Redlands

Charlotte Jones has written seven previous stage plays: *Airswimming, In Flame, Martha, Josie and the Chinese Elvis, Humble Boy, The Dark, The Lightning Play* and *The Meeting*. She won the Critics' Circle Most Promising Playwright Award, 1999. *Martha, Josie and the Chinese Elvis* won the Pearson TV Best New Play Award and Manchester Evening News Best New Play Award, 1999. *Humble Boy* won the Critics' Circle Best New Play, 2001, Susan Smith Blackburn Award, People's Choice Best New Play, 2001, and was nominated for an Olivier Award and a Drama Desk Award. It ran at the National Theatre and in the West End and has since been produced all over the world. She wrote the book for Andrew Lloyd Webber's musical of Wilkie Collins' novel *The Woman in White* (lyrics by David Zippel) which ran in the West End and on Broadway. She has also written extensively for TV, film and radio. She is an Honorary Fellow of Balliol College, Oxford.

by the same author

CHARLOTTE JONES: PLAYS I
(*Airswimming, In Flame,
Martha, Josie and the Chinese Elvis, Humble Boy*)

THE DARK
HUMBLE BOY
THE LIGHTNING PLAY
THE MEETING

CHARLOTTE JONES

Redlands

faber

First published in 2024
by Faber and Faber Limited
The Bindery, 51 Hatton Garden
London, EC1N 8HN

Typeset by Brighton Gray
Printed and bound in the UK by CPI Group (Ltd), Croydon CR0 4YY

All rights reserved
© Charlotte Jones, 2024

Charlotte Jones is hereby identified as author
of this work in accordance with Section 77 of the
Copyright, Designs and Patents Act 1988

All rights whatsoever in this work, amateur or professional,
are strictly reserved. Applications for permission for any use
whatsoever including performance rights must be made in
advance, prior to any such proposed use,
to Casarotto Ramsay & Associates, 3rd Floor, 7 Savoy Court,
Strand, London WC2R 0EX

No performance may be given unless a licence
has first been obtained

This book is sold subject to the condition that it shall not,
by way of trade or otherwise, be lent, resold, hired out
or otherwise circulated without the publisher's prior consent
in any form of binding or cover other than that in which
it is published and without a similar condition including
this condition being imposed on the subsequent purchaser

A CIP record for this book
is available from the British Library

ISBN 978-0-571-39498-2

Printed and bound in the UK on FSC® certified paper in line with our continuing
commitment to ethical business practices, sustainability and the environment.
For further information see faber.co.uk/environmental-policy

2 4 6 8 10 9 7 5 3 1

Redlands was first performed at Chichester Festival Theatre on 20 September 2024, with the following cast:

Constable Flint / Daphne / News Reporter
  Melody Chikakane Brown
Michael Havers QC Anthony Calf
English Teacher / George Harrison / Allen Klein /
  Newscaster / Radio Announcer Ben Caplan
Cecil Havers Clive Francis
Nigel Havers Louis Landau
Dancer / Frieda Lara Rose McCabe
Marianne Faithfull Emer McDaid
Keith Richards Brenock O'Connor
Chief Inspector Bramley / Judge Block / RADA Principal
  Sam Pay
Carol Havers Olivia Poulet
PC Willis / Vivek Chakrabarti Akshay Sharan
Mick Jagger Japer Talbot
Pattie Boyd / Sheila / Shop Assistant / Female Fan /
  Journalist / Drama Student Ella Tekere
Dancer / Hawker / Policeman / Newspaper Seller /
  Appeal Clerk Riley Woodford
Sniderman / Philip Havers / Terry / Derek Carter /
  Cricket Commentator Adam Young

All other roles played by members of the company.

Director Justin Audibert
Set Designer Joanna Scotcher
Costume Designer Ryan Dawson Laight
Lighting Designer Matt Daw
Composer and Orchestrator Benjamin Kwasi Burrell
Sound Designer Claire Windsor
Musical Director Alan Berry
Movement Director Shannelle 'Tali' Fergus
Casting Director Ginny Schiller CDG
Associate Director Julia Head
Associate Musical Director Joshua Griffith

For Lindsey Jones, my dad,
who taught me to love Rock 'n' Roll.

Characters

Nigel Havers
seventeen

Michael Havers
Nigel's father, fifties

Carol Havers
Nigel's mother, forties

Mick Jagger

Keith Richards

Marianne Faithfull

George Harrison

Pattie Boyd
George's wife

Sniderman

PC Willis

Chief Inspector Gordon Bramley
fifties

Constable Rosemary Flint
forties

Daphne
fifties

Vivek Chakrabarti
twenties

Allen Klein
early forties

High Court Judge Cecil Havers
Michael's father

Philip Havers
Michael and Carol's older son, nineteen

Sheila *and* **Frieda**
secretaries

Terry
a macho photographer in his twenties

Judge Block
fifties/sixties

Derek Carter
a London hack, thirties

English Teacher
Schoolboys
Female Usher
Police Officers
Hip Shop Assistant
Male Usher
Female News Reporter
Fans
Cricket Commentator
Cricket Player
Court Clerk
Prison Guards
Journalist
Radio Announcer
Waiter
Drama Student
Principal of RADA

REDLANDS

Note

This is a fictionalised account, inspired by the famous
'Redlands' trial of the Rolling Stones.

Act One

SCENE ONE

A young, pretty, blond-haired man of seventeen walks onto the stage. He looks at the audience and smiles. He is a little nervous.

Nigel Hello. Hi. You don't know me yet . . . but my name is Nigel Havers. And one day I am going to be famous. Well maybe not famous, but I'm going to be an actor. I mean, I'd very much like to be an actor. There's only one problem –

A camp English Teacher walks on.

English Teacher Havers! Havers! We need your help!

Nigel (*to the audience*) So right now, I'm still at school. A minor public school, in, for argument's sake, let's say Chichester. So it's February 1967. And I want you to imagine that this is the moment, the actual moment when I know I must be an actor. Here on this very stage.

Other schoolboys walk on. They carry bits of set which they start to place around Nigel.
They are singing quietly: the opening chorus of 'You Can Make It If You Try' by Ted Jarrett.
Nigel proceeds to warm up for his performance.

English Teacher Havers!

Nigel Yes, sir!

English Teacher We need you in the forest!

Nigel goes to go and turns back to the audience.

Nigel (*to the audience*) We're doing *A Midsummer Night's Dream*. It's by William Shakespeare. But you knew that, of course –

He looks at the set being assembled around him. We see the first suggestion of Keith Richards' country house: Redlands. Baronial and pop art design combined. A battered leather sofa. Hanging Turkish lamps, Andy Warhol cushions, a low table.

(*To the audience.*) It's a very modern production.

English Teacher These lamps will represent our trees.

Nigel (*to the audience*) I can tell you now, my dad is going to absolutely hate it.

English Teacher Havers! Please help the choir!

Nigel Coming, sir!

Nigel takes a last look at the audience.

And that's the problem, you see – my . . . No! I'm not going to say it – what do we say in the theatre? *Show*, don't *tell*!

English Teacher Havers!

Nigel Here, sir!

English Teacher We all have to pull our weight – even when we've been lucky enough to be offered a starring role.

Nigel Yes, sir!

The set is almost complete. Nigel helps with the finishing touches.

English Teacher Good. Yes. Very avant-garde! Ready?

Nigel I just hope I'm good enough.

English Teacher Showtime, boys!! Lights and action!

The lights change and Nigel takes his position on stage as Puck. The English Teacher is barely concealed in the wings, mouthing along with all the words.

Nigel (*as Puck*)
   The King doth keep his revels here tonight.
   Take heed the Queen come not within his sight,
   For Oberon is passing fell and wrath –

   There is a commotion at the back of the theatre.

   Because that she, as her attendant, hath
   A lovely boy stolen from an Indian king.
   She never had so sweet a changeling.
   And jealous Oberon would have the child –

   Michael Havers, a handsome man in his fifties, is entering at the back of the auditorium. He is talking to the Female Usher, too loudly.

Michael Yes, I'm terribly, sorry, I got held up at the Old Bailey. Oh, has it started? Darn it.

Female Usher Can I see your ticket, Mr Havers?

Michael Oh, my wife deals with that.

Female Usher That's fine.

Michael I haven't missed much, have I?

Female Usher No, no, sir, just follow me.

   The Usher leads Michael down the stairs.

Nigel (*to the audience*) This is exactly what I'm talking about.

Michael I can't see a bloody thing! I'm going to break my neck.

English Teacher (*to the lighting box*) Hello in the box! Tarquin! Could we put some lights on for Mr Havers?

Michael Ah! Would you be so kind? Oh, that's much better.

Nigel (*to the audience*) He drives me insane.

At the front of the theatre, sitting in the auditorium is Carol Havers, attractive, forties. She stands up in her seat.

Carol For God's sake, Michael! What's wrong with you?

Michael I'm coming! I'm coming! It's only a school play for God's sake. Sorry. Excuse me. I do beg your pardon.

Michael stops to greet a member of the audience.

(*Improvised.*) Oh hello! Nice to see you! And is this your lovely mother/wife? How are you?

Nigel (*to audience*) He's always like this.

Carol Michael! Get here at once.

Female Usher Your seat is at the end of the front row, sir.

Michael Very good.

Michael (*as he makes his way to his seat, to the audience*) Terribly sorry about all this. Tricky case at the Old Bailey today. Obscenity case. We were asked to consider whether the latest production at the National Theatre of Great Britain contravened Section Thirteen of the Sexual Offences act. Terrible play of course –

Carol Michael. Nigel is *acting*!

Nigel
 And jealous Oberon would have the child –

Michael notices his son on stage.

Michael Oh, so he is!

He turns to a member of the audience, by way of clarification.

That's my son.

He takes in the set.

Oh Lord, it's not modern dress, is it?

Nigel (*to the audience*) Didn't I tell you?

English Teacher Yes, I just thought – I am a great devotee of Peter Brook, Mr Havers. The empty space –

Michael I just don't understand why you have to meddle with things.

Carol (*to Michael*) That's enough. Stop talking and sit down immediately!

Michael All right, woman. I've had a very taxing day.

Carol Well, you don't have to make a song and dance of it.

He sits down. Nigel is staring at him.

Nigel (*to his father*) Have you quite finished?

Michael Is he talking to me?

Carol Of course he's talking to you.

English Teacher (*stage whisper*) Tarquin! House lights please!

Michael Can he do that? He's breaking the fourth wall, Carol.

Carol It's Shakespeare. It's allowed.

Michael Are you sure about that?

Carol If you don't shut up, I'll be breaking a lot more than the fourth wall –

English Teacher I SAID HOUSE LIGHTS!

The house lights snap out.

Nigel I'm afraid to say, Dad, our revels are not ended, not by a long shot. I hope you won't be offended – but I have a feeling you will be. You always are. Because tonight, this very night, not seven miles from here, in a place called West Wittering –

Nigel turns to the audience.

Do you know it? . . . Tonight in a house called 'Redlands', there are some other merry wanderers of the night. I think you should meet them. Yes! And because this is theatre and in theatre anything is possible, I say: let the visions appear!

Nigel claps his hands.

SCENE TWO

Lights change. They become kaleidoscopic. Music.
 Into the 'forest' set tumble Mick Jagger, Keith Richards and Marianne Faithfull. They are beautiful and dressed to the hippy nines. They stand there a moment as if they are young lovers, lost in the forest.
 Michael and Carol get up to leave the auditorium, bickering.

Michael Is that it then?

Carol Yes! We're leaving and I'm driving.

Michael I really should just pop and say hello to the headmaster –

Carol No, Michael! You've done enough damage for one night.

They leave.
 On stage music starts up and the characters 'awaken'.
 We're at a laid-back party at Keith's country house, Redlands. Post acid-trip. Two of the partygoers are George Harrison, the Beatle, and his wife Pattie Boyd. Nigel looks at them for a moment and then runs off.

George Nice pad you got here, Keith.

Keith Redlands? Yeah. I was lookin' at some other houses and I just drove up here by mistake – you know, poncin' about in my Bentley. But the moment I saw her – Grade Two listed, thatched roof, moat – I knew I had to have her. Love at first sight. I said, 'I'm gonna buy this house,' didn't I, Mick?

Mick You certainly did. And I said, ain't it a bit posh for you, mate?

Keith And I said nah! It needs a bit of me to balance it out. So you know what I did, George?

George No. What did you do, Keith?

Keith I went right up and knocked on the door. And this old geezer comes out –

Mick Very pukka, you know –

Keith Ex-commodore of the Royal Navy no less. Mr Hoity-Toity and me in my leathers. And I says: I'm looking to buy a house, but I made a wrong turning – and he said –

Mick (*posh accent*) 'What you need is Piggery Hall Lane' –

Keith And I says: 'But what about this place? Is this for sale?' And he says:

Mick 'Well there's no sign up, but it could be for sale.'

Keith And I looked at him and I said: 'How much, guvnor?'

Mick 'Twenty thousand English pounds, my good man' –

Keith Thinking that'll scare me off, like. And so I says 'What time is it?' – cool as you like – and he says –

Mick 'One o'clock.' And course the banks are only open till three.

Keith So, I says: 'Are you by any chance going to be in later?'

Mick 'Why yes, of course.'

Keith 'If I bring you twenty grand in cash, do we have a deal?'

Mick 'I don't see why not. But I want it agreed by this evening or it's off.'

George Old school. I like it.

Keith Right! So I zoomed up to London, just got to the bank in time, got the bread –

Mick Twenty grand in a brown paper bag!

Keith And by the evening I was sitting in front of the fire, signing the deeds.

George Nice one, Keith.

Keith I bloody love this place. Suits me, don't it?

Marianne It suits me better of course as I am descended from aristocracy.

Keith Ooh Lady Muck!

Marianne It's true!

Mick Yeah, you're proper posh, baby.

Pattie I didn't know that about you, Marianne.

Marianne Oh yes, Pattie, my mother is a baroness. Habsburg dynasty. We did things in the war.

Pattie Groovy!

Marianne goes to go.

Mick Where you going, babe?

Marianne I got so cold at the beach, I'm going to take a bath.

Mick Want me to join?

Marianne What a good idea!

Keith Mick! Let her take a bath, for Pete's sake! Our Marianne is a very dirty girl.

Marianne Piss off, Keith!

Keith Language, Marianne!

She leaves.

(*To Mick.*) Look at you, all googly eyed! Been drinkin' the love juice, mate?

Mick Fuck off.

Keith Nah, don't get me wrong, I don't blame you. If you get tired of her, send her my way.

Mick You wish. You're not her type, mate.

They laugh companionably.

George (*Scouse accent*) Keith. Me and Pattie need to be gettin' off now.

Keith What you talkin' about? The night is young!

Mick Come on, man, we're only just getting going –

George Sorry, Mick. Paul's got us in the studio early.

Keith Come here then, Georgie boy. Give us a smacker!

They all say their goodbyes. Overlapping.

George Stay cool, Keith.

Keith Always, mate.

Mick Bye, Pattie love. See you soon yeah.

Pattie Bye, Mick. Say bye to Marianne for me.

Keith Bye, Pats.

Pattie Bye, Keith.

Mick Georgie boy!

George See you soon, mate.

George and Pattie leave.

Keith Christ, I thought they'd never go! Let's get the party started!

Keith clicks his finger and the music changes.

That's more like it! Let's be having you! Come on, Mick. Get off your arse! Show us some moves!

Keith and Mick get up and start clapping and cavorting to the music.
Suddenly a young man flies through the 'window' as if propelled. He falls in a heap on the floor in front of Keith and Mick. He carries an attaché case. The music stops. They both stare at the intruder.

Mick What the –

Keith Where did he come from? Did you invite anyone else?

Mick Nope. Seems like we've got ourselves an intruder.

Keith (*to the young man*) Oi! I'll have you know that I'm the lord of this particular manor and I don't hold with gatecrashers –

The intruder gets up.

Sniderman (*Canadian accent*) Don't be like that, Keith.

Keith Do I know you?

Sniderman Yeah, sure! You know me! We've met a bunch of times! They called me the Mad Hatter then.

Keith goes and looks at him more closely.

Keith Sniderman?! Is that you? Look, Mick! It's Sniderman, as I live and breathe!

Mick Fuck me! Is this a dream?

Sniderman No dream, Mick! Here at your service!

Mick Yay! The Acid King is in our midst!

Sniderman The very same!

Keith What the fuck you doin' in West Wittering?

Sniderman I come bearing gifts!

Sniderman clicks the lock on the attaché case. The case flips open and concertinas down, full of druggy treasures. He displays it as a travelling salesman would.

Voilà! I got a whole psycho-delicatessen just for you. Look at this. I got zoomers, pixies, kitty flip, beans, flake, roll, bliss, crank, zip, bump, spice, dots and everyone's favourite, a little bit of wonky. You name it. I got it. Purple haze, purple hearts, purple drank. Whatever you want. I got all your mushrooms, freshly picked today. Oh and Vicks 44. For that lickle tickle in your throat. I got it all, man. Your juice and your beans. Gear to take you up, gear to take you down . . . And something for the inevitable munchies afterwards. Nosh nosh nosh. Don't say I didn't think of everything.

Keith I think I love you.

At this point Marianne re-enters wearing nothing but a fur rug.

Marianne What have I missed?

Mick The ice-cream man, darlin'.

Marianne Oh goody! I'm feeling a bit peckish.

Sniderman Hello, Marianne. Like the rug.

Marianne I wear it well, don't I? So come on, what have you got for me?

Sniderman takes out a bottle of orange tablets.

Sniderman (*reverently*) For you, Marianne: tonight's special. The Tao of Dimethyltryptamine. It will help you navigate the cosmos!

Marianne Oh! I was born to navigate the cosmos.

Sniderman Don't I know it!

Keith What the hell are we waiting for then!

Laughter. Sniderman starts handing out goodies. Everyone starts to smoke and ingest. The party gets increasingly spaced out as a very young police officer, PC Willis, runs on stage and enters a phone box. He puts some coins in the slot.

Willis Hello? Inspector? This is PC Trevor Willis reporting from Redlands Lane. George Harrison and his lovely wife Pattie have left the building! He just drove out in a cream Mini Cooper. I repeat – the Beatle has flown! . . . What? Wait a minute, sir –

He desperately puts more coins in the slot.

(*Affronted.*) Yeah! Of course it was George Harrison! I think I know a Beatle when I see one – Inspector? Are you still there? Inspector?!

But his coins have run out.
   A police whistle. At this, other police officers run on stage, surrounding the 'house'. They are led by Chief Inspector Gordon Bramley, a joyless man in his fifties, aided by his right-hand woman, Constable Rosemary Flint, forties, stern.

Bramley Are we ready, Constable Flint?

Flint Never been more ready, Chief Inspector.

Bramley This is it then, Rosemary.

Flint Lead the way, Gordon.

Bramley Let's get the long-haired louts!

Bramley lifts a loudspeaker to his lips. Flint turns to her men.

Flint Get down, men!

The other police officers crouch, ready for the raid.

Bramley (*through a loudhailer*) THIS IS A POLICE RAID! OPEN UP!

Marianne Oh my God!

Mick What the fuck was that?

Keith Don't you worry! I've got this –

He stands unsteadily and wobbles towards the 'door'. Stoned.

Mick Hey, mate! You can't do this on your own. I'm coming with you –

Marianne Can I come too?

Mick We've got this, babe.

Marianne No, I think I'd better come.

Bramley (*through the loudhailer*) I REPEAT: THIS IS A POLICE RAID! OPEN UP AND LET US IN!

Keith That was very loud.

Marianne Is it a game?! Do you think we should hide?

Mick Nah, nah, let's check it out! Keith, look through the keyhole!

Keith Good idea, man. Like it.

Marianne Be careful, Keith.

Keith stoops unsteadily to look through the 'keyhole'.

Keith Fuck me.

Marianne What is it?!

Mick What can you see?

Keith You're not going to believe this – but there's a bunch of really little people out there.

Marianne Really?!

Mick Wooooooooh.

Keith Yeah. All dressed in the same clothes.

Marianne How enchanting!

Mick Are they leprechauns, Keith?

Keith In Sussex? I don't think so.

Marianne What are they doing? Look again!

Keith does so.

Keith They're just sort of – in the bushes.

Marianne Are they frolicking?

Keith Yeah! You know what. I think they're fairies.

Mick Wow! I bloody love fairies.

Keith Me too.

Marianne I was a fairy in another life.

Bramley (*through the loudhailer*) IF YOU DO NOT OPEN THE DOOR, WE WILL BE FORCED TO BREAK IT DOWN!

Marianne Keith. I think they want to come in!

Keith What should we do about the fairies?

Mick It's cold out there, Keith.

Marianne Oh yes, they must be frozen, poor little things.

Keith Right. Right.

Mick We should let the little people warm themselves by the fire.

Marianne We can befriend them!

Keith YEAH!

Keith opens the door.

Hello, my little ones! Hail!

Mick Hail!

Marianne Hail! We are mortal! But don't be scared.

Keith You are all most welcome! Aah! Will you look at the lovely band of fairies!

Marianne They're all so magical!

Mick Beautiful.

Keith We should communicate with them.

Mick Show them we mean no harm. But how?

Keith Don't worry. I speak a bit of fairy. Eeh eeh eeh eeh!

Mick Eeh! Eeh!

Marianne No, no it's more like this. Ah-ah-ah-ah-ah.

Flint Gordon, what are they doing?

Bramley I've no idea, Rosemary. But I don't like it.

Flint Just stick to the script, Inspector. You can do this.

Bramley (*to Keith*) Are you Mr Keith Richards?

Keith You already know my name? I love that.

Flint That's him. That's Richards! That's Jagger. And she's the girl!

Bramley And this, ladies and gentlemen, is a police raid.

Marianne I think they may be trying to tell us something.

Mick Yeah, actually, I don't think they're fairies, Keith.

Marianne No, maybe not.

Mick and Marianne back off.

Bramley (*to Keith*) Are you the owner and occupier of the premises?

Keith You're so sweet!

Bramley I am not sweet. I am Inspector Gordon Bramley of the West Sussex Constabulary and I have a warrant to search these premises under the Dangerous Drugs Act of 1965.

Flint blows her police whistle very loudly. Keith, Mick and Marianne flinch.

Flint MEN!!

The police officers leap to their feet and invade the house. Pandemonium.

Keith Wo, wo, wo. What is this? Hold on a minute!

Marianne screams and pulls the fur rug tightly around her.

Marianne Mick!

Mick Fuck!

Keith What do you think you're doing?

Mick goes and put his arm around Marianne. Sniderman grabs up his attaché case and leaps back out of the 'window'.

Flint Smells funny in here, doesn't it?

Keith That's joss sticks, mate!

Bramley (*to Keith*) I'll give you joss sticks. Men!

The police officers start to dismantle the 'set' – carry off cushions and lamps etc.

Bramley That's it. Take anything suspicious. Bag it all up!

Flint goes to Mick, who is comforting Marianne.

Flint Oi, you. That's enough of that. Get your dirty hands off her.

Marianne But what if I like it?

Flint Good God, man. Are you wearing make-up?

Mick Are *you* wearing make-up?

Flint What?

Marianne You really should! It would take years off you.

Mick She's right, you know.

Flint How dare you! Willis! Take this deviant out of my sight.

Flint looks at Marianne.

I've been sent to deal with you, young lady.

Marianne I bet you have.

Flint What exactly are you wearing?

Marianne I can't be sure, but I think it's rabbit.

Flint Don't be disgusting.

Bramley I want full body searches! Hands in the air!

Marianne Are you certain you want me to do that?

Flint You heard what the Inspector said.

Marianne I'm not wearing anything underneath but okay.

Flint Cease! Desist!

Bramley Common decency at all times!

Marianne What's the matter, don't you like what you see? Suit yourself, babes.

Willis searches Mick.

Willis (*to Mick*) I've got all your records you know.

They high-five.

Mick Nice. Let me know if you want them signed.

Willis Really?! Thank you. Sorry about this.

Bramley Willis!

Another Police Officer runs on with a tin which he proudly presents to Bramley.

Police Officer Inspector. I found this in the kitchen!

Bramley smells it.

Bramley Very suspicious.

Keith That's Earl Grey, mate. Very nice with a bit of lemon.

Bramley Bag it up!

At this point Willis finds a plastic bag with four blue pills in Mick's inner jacket pocket.

Willis Inspector!

Mick Oh shit.

Marianne Mick?!

Keith Whoopsy.

Bramley rushes over and grabs the bag, holds it up to the light.

Bramley Oh dear, oh dear oh dear oh dear. What do we have here then?

Mick and Keith exchange a glance.

Haha! I think we got what we came for. Step down, men!

Bramley walks up to Mick and Keith.

What have you got to say for yourselves now then?

The boys look at each other. They sing the first two verses and chorus of 'Not Fade Away' by Buddy Holly to the astonished policemen. The police snap to and Mick and Keith are placed in handcuffs and led off, as:

SCENE THREE

Michael's study, at his country farmhouse home, White Shutters. Evening.
Michael sits at his desk, in his swivel chair, as he pours a glass of whisky. On the desk is a wig stand with a lawyer's wig on it. The radio is on.

Newscaster (*radio*) West Sussex Constabulary have tonight confirmed that Mr Mick Jagger and Mr Keith Richards, both of the Rolling Stones, have been charged under various sections of the Dangerous Drugs Act.

Michael Ha!

Newscaster (*radio*) Both men are called to attend a hearing at Chichester Magistrates' Court on Monday.

Michael Serves them right. Degenerate swine.

Carol enters. Michael switches off the radio.

(*Indicating his glass.*) Hello, darling, care to join me?

Carol I'm going to bed now.

Michael Little nightcap?

Carol I'm exhausted.

Michael Toast my success in court today?

Carol Michael, I want you to apologise to Nigel.

Michael What?

Carol It was very rude of you.

Michael I wasn't that late!

Carol And tell him he was good.

Michael Was he good?

Carol He was excellent in the play. Everyone said so.

Michael Did they? Well, that's all very well, I just hope it's not going to interfere with his schoolwork –

Carol Michael, for heaven's sake –

Michael Can't you talk to him?

Carol Not this time, no.

Michael Please Carol, I find it difficult to know what to say – you know what he's like –

Carol You have to remember that he is not a hostile witness, he is your son. And he's very sensitive.

Michael Sensitive! We'd all like to be sensitive!

Carol You know what I think? You and Nigel are more alike than you let on.

Pause.

The play meant a lot to him. Promise me you'll make an effort. You'll feel better for it.

Sound of door slamming.

That will be him. Michael!

Michael Yes, yes, yes, all right.

Carol I'll send him through.

She goes to go.

And don't forget to take the dog out for his last wee.

She leaves. Michael grumbles to himself as he pours himself another drink. After a moment Nigel enters and stands awkwardly in the doorway.

Michael Ah! Nigel.

Nigel You wanted to see me?

Pause.

Michael Please take a seat.

Nigel I'd rather stand.

Michael I see.

Pause.

Well. I was a little late for your – erm, yes. But I was involved in a very important case today. At the Old Bailey.

Nigel You said.

Pause.

Michael Right up your street in fact. It had to do with this play on at the National. There's a scene in it – where they simulate an act of – where two men – in a state of undress – attempt to – well it doesn't matter exactly what they were up to. Something ungodly. But basically, the Prosecution was trying to suggest that any criminal act depicted on the English stage should be liable for prosecution!

Pause.

I said by those standards any actor playing Hamlet should be up for mass murder! Let's get Larry Olivier in the stand I said! The Judge loved that. I mean, the case made no sense! The average bloke on the Clapham omnibus would have seen straight through it. They were trying to make a mockery of the Law and I won't have that! I mean I saw the play and it was utter rubbish from beginning to end. But then most theatre is, isn't it?

Nigel Can I go now please?

Pause.

Michael Just one moment.

Michael goes to the wig on his desk.

You see this. This was my first. I bought it from Ede and Ravenscroft of course. You know, on Chancery Lane. There were two different types. I remember I asked the assistant – why is that one so much more expensive than the other? And you know what he said?

Pause.

He said: that one is made from the mane of the horse. But this one is made from the horse's tail. And I said: But I thought the mane hair would be more expensive? And you know what he said?

After a moment Nigel shakes his head.

It costs more to prepare the horse's tail, sir. And I still didn't get it, you see and so he spelled it out to me: the tail hair has to be cleaned more thoroughly, sir, because it's so full of shit!

Michael laughs.

SO FULL OF SHIT!!

Nigel smiles weakly.

You know, Nigel, seeing you tonight, up on the – doing your – in those – tights – I was thinking to myself – I don't see you in criminal law somehow. I think corporate law may be more your thing – those boys earn a bloody packet!

Nigel (*quietly*) I don't think I want to be a lawyer.

Pause.

Michael Anyway, good chat! You must be tired. After all that. Yes. Early start tomorrow. Don't worry, I'll see to the dog.

Michael leaves. Nigel looks at the audience. During this speech he undoes his tie and loosens his collar.

Nigel (*sadly, to the audience*) You see, everyone in my family is a lawyer. My dad – he's a very big deal. They say he'll make Attorney General one day. And my aunt is going to be the first ever female judge. Elizabeth Butler-Sloss. She's absolutely terrifying. And Bongo – that's my grandfather – he's called Cecil but we all call him Bongo. Bongo was the judge for Ruth Ellis, the last woman in this country to be, well, hanged. I'm rather afraid if I become an actor, I might go the same way.

He messes up his hair and runs off.

SCENE FOUR

Chambers. Day.
We are in the reception at the Inner Temple. A suggestion of a typing pool. Michael enters.

Secretaries Morning, Mr Havers!

He ignores them. He is met by a breathless Daphne, a matronly woman in her fifties.

Daphne Mr Havers, I'm terribly sorry but there's a man in your office – a rather – peculiar man – in a state of frankly I don't know what –

Michael Stop it, Daphne. You're being shrill. I will see to it.

Daphne Yes, Mr Havers.

He goes to his desk. Vivek Chakrabarti, a more junior barrister (Indian, twenties) is arguing with a short, barrel-chested man.

Vivek I'm afraid you cannot come in here without an appointment and certainly not without a solicitor –

Michael Thank you, Mr Chakrabarti, I will deal with this –

Allen I told you it won't take a minute!

Allen Klein is a man in his early forties, very New York, with extravagant hair. He is injecting himself in the leg with a syringe.

Michael Good God, man! Could you be any more depraved? I don't know what this is. But I won't have it! Not in the Inner Temple!

Allen It's a pleasure to meet you too.

Allen puts away the syringe in a tin.

It's insulin by the way.

Allen puts the small tin back into his pocket.

Vivek I believe that Mr Klein is a diabetic.

Michael Yes, yes, I know what insulin is!

Allen (*to Michael*) Blood sugar too high – needed a jab. I try to be discreet about these things – people can so easily jump to the wrong conclusions –

Michael I see. Quite. Yes, Mr –

Allen Klein. Allen Klein.

Michael I'm sorry. Do we know each other?

Vivek Mr Klein is the manager of a 'rock band' –

Allen Not any old rock band – the Rolling Stones!

Michael is unmoved. Allen offers him his hand.

And you're the best, I hear. And believe me, I only deal with the best.

Michael does not shake it.

Michael You can speak to my secretary, arrange an appointment through your solicitor –

Allen Do you mind if I take a seat? I can feel a little woozy as it hits my bloodstream –

He does so.

So, you may have heard my boys got themselves in a spot of bother. And guess what, it's your lucky day! I've chosen you to represent them.

Michael I'm afraid it doesn't work like that –

Allen I loved what you did with the obscenity case. You know the play. 'Is this a penis that I see before me?'

Pause.

I saw that, and I thought, this guy understands showbusiness!

Pause.

(*To Vivek.*) Hey, pal, show him the gubbins –

Vivek This is the deposition, sir –

Vivek hands Michael the case deposition.

Michael This is just a preliminary hearing. I don't deal with this sort of thing, Mr . . .

Allen Klein –

Michael Mr Klein – why don't you speak to my junior counsel here: Mr Chakrabarti. I'm afraid I can't waste my time with this –

Allen This won't end at the magistrates' court, believe me. Look. Everyone loves the Beatles, right? The Beatles wanna

hold your hand, but my boys – they wanna fuck your –
I mean it's all 'mothers, lock up your daughters', you know
what I'm saying?

Michael You make yourself very clear.

Allen You got daughters, Havers?

Michael Two sons.

Allen Baruch HaShem! Look, the boys want you, they don't want anyone else. I'm begging you – I'm not a well man and the strain this is putting on me! Please just take a look –

Michael sighs and sits. He looks at the case deposition again.

Michael Mr Jagger is being charged with the possession of amphetamine sulphate and methyl hydrochloride –

Allen A little bit of Benzedrine, that's all – every housewife's friend, huh?

Michael Not any housewife with whom I am acquainted.

Allen No but thing is he got it on prescription.

Michael He did?

Allen Well, more or less.

Michael looks at him and then looks back at the deposition.

Michael And Mr Richards is being charged with – what exactly?

Allen Owning the place. The house – Redlands. How crazy is that? Just because he ain't some fancy Lord –

Michael More illegal substances were found on the property, I understand?

Allen A few joints. A tab or two of acid. The teeniest bit of speed. 'You ain't hip till you trip.' Isn't that what they say?

Allen laughs. But he is met with stony-faced disapproval.

Michael Do Mr Jagger and Mr Richards have any prior convictions?

Allen No. No. Absolutely not. They're clean. I mean. There was an incident a while back. Boys being boys.

Michael Enlighten me.

Allen Well –

Michael Yes?

Allen They were caught urinating in a garage.

Michael I don't think this is for me.

Michael closes the deposition and pushes it away.

Allen No, no, no, no, no. You don't understand. My boys are about to hit America. If they go to jail, they won't be able to tour – this case could end their careers!

Michael I'm very sorry to disappoint you.

Pause.

Allen Look, Havers. I'm gonna shoot from the hip now. This set-up you've got here – it's all very nice and everything in its ye olde worlde Ebenezer Scrooge kinda way but I'm talking about rock and roll! You could seriously make a name for yourself with this.

Michael I already have a name for myself, thank you very much. Good day to you.

SCENE FIVE

Theatre.
Nigel enters from another part of the auditorium. He speaks to the audience.

Nigel Okay, so strictly speaking, I should be at school. But what I reckon is, I don't need to pass any exams, not if I'm going to be an actor. And as you already know, the theatre is my second home.

We see a sign indicating that this is the Royal Court Theatre.

Plus, I was so lucky to get a last-minute ticket. I couldn't pass that up.

He takes a seat. Turns to the audience member next to him.

Excuse me. Could I borrow your programme for a moment?

He either does or doesn't take a programme.

(*Improvised.*) Thanks so much. I just wanted to check something. / No, they're so expensive, aren't they? Daylight robbery.

Pause.

Thanks. Marianne Faithfull is playing Nina.

He hands the programme back, if necessary.

It's the first time I've seen any Chekhov.

Marianne Faithfull runs on as Nina in The Seagull. *She's wearing a mini-dress. She pauses a moment.*

(*To the audience.*) It's a modern production! Brilliant!

Nigel watches transfixed.

Marianne (*as Nina*) Why do you say you kiss the ground I walk on?

Nigel Because I do. I would. If given the chance.

Marianne (*as Nina*) I ought to be killed.

Nigel No!

Marianne (*as Nina*) I'm so tired, Kostya! If I could only rest . . . rest . . . I am the seagull . . . No, that's not it. I'm an actress.

Nigel stands up in his seat and applauds her.

Nigel Bravo, Marianne! Bravo!

Lights change. Nigel goes on stage.

(*To audience.*) I made a bit of a tit of myself there.

Marianne turns away.

Miss Faithfull! Miss Faithfull! Please may I have your autograph?

He turns back to the audience.

(*To the audience.*) Don't worry, I'm fast-forwarding a bit. The play's actually finished. I'm at the stage door now.

Marianne gathers up her bag, a large hat and sunglasses. She turns back to Nigel.

I have a pen!

Marianne Do you have a programme?

Nigel No, sorry, I couldn't afford one.

She takes his arm.

Marianne This will have to do then.

She signs it.

Marianne Faithfull. Kiss.

She blows on his arm to dry the ink.

Marianne There, I hope you're never going to wash again.

Nigel No, absolutely not . . . Scout's honour.

Marianne DYB, DYB, DYB!

Nigel turns to the audience.

Nigel (*to the audience*) I'm an idiot.

He turns back to her.

You're such a good actress!

Marianne No I'm not! I've had terrible reviews. 'Marianne Faithfull looks the part even if she can't get much out of the words.'

Nigel What do the critics know? Bunch of old codgers.

Pause.

Marianne Words are very important to me, as a matter of fact . . . It's a curse being pretty, really it is. No one takes you seriously.

Nigel Oh I think you're marvellous.

Marianne Do you really?

Nigel Absolutely.

Marianne You're very sweet.

Nigel Thank you very much.

Marianne What's your name?

Nigel Havers, Nigel Havers.

Marianne Well Havers, Nigel Havers, do you want to come shopping with me?

Nigel What?

Marianne Let's hit the town!

Nigel turns to the audience.

Nigel I mean is this *actually* happening? I think she must feel sorry for me or something. It can't be that she actually likes me – I'm nobody – and she's –

Marianne Well?

He turns back to her.

Nigel I mean that's such a kind offer – but –

Marianne But what? You need to be back at school? Oh, don't let me stop you –

Nigel No, no, I don't. I'd like that. Shopping, yes. I love to shop.

She looks at him.

Marianne I really think we need to change your vibe.

Nigel Oh yes, I agree. I loathe my vibe.

Marianne We should do something about this hair.

She runs her hands through his hair.

Nigel (*to the audience*) Oh crikey.

Marianne Well? Are we going or what?

Nigel Yes, please absolutely we're going thank you very much.

Music. King's Road, London.
  Nigel follows Marianne, as if he is having a hallucinogenic trip. Hippies appear and disappear. Marianne and the ensemble sing the choruses and first two verses of 'Going to a Go-Go' by Smokey Robinson and the Miracles.

They arrive at their destination. A shop: Granny Takes a Trip. A Hip Shop Assistant rolls on a rack of clothes. Marianne rifles through them. Nigel stands stiffly by her. She picks out three or four very bright shirts.

Marianne (*to Shop Assistant*) He'll try them all.

Nigel I will?

Shop Assistant (*taking the clothes from her*) Yes, anything you say, Miss Faithfull!

Nigel looks at Marianne.

Marianne Go on then.

Nigel Yes, sorry. Of course. Thanks.

He follows the Hip Shop Assistant. He takes one last look at Marianne as she takes out a tin. He goes back to her.

Erm. Will you wait? I mean – will you still be here when I come back out?

She smiles.

Marianne We'll just have to see, won't we?

He takes another last look at her and exits. As she smokes, the vision of King's Road disappears.

SCENE SIX

White Shutters, kitchen.
Sunday lunch. Carol brings on a roasting tray and sets it on the table. Michael enters and stands at the head of the table. He stares at the meat.

Michael I need my – implements. Carol?!

She sighs demonstrably. She runs off and collects the carving knife and fork. She slams the implements in front of him.

Carol Do I have to do everything round here?

Michael Well, I have no idea where they live, do I?

Carol (*sotto voce*) Only been here for twenty years. Why on earth would you know?

Carol goes to shout for the others.

Lunch is ready, everyone!

Michael starts to sharpen the carving knife. Two guests enter and take their seats at the table. Michael's father, High Court Judge Cecil Havers – a handsome, silver-haired man, seventies – and Philip, the Havers' older son, nineteen. He wears a Corpus Christi College rowing sweatshirt. Carol is bustling around placing hot plates of vegetables on the table.

Cecil Thank you, Carol.

Philip Thanks, Ma.

Cecil So, Philip, how are you enjoying Cambridge?

Philip Very much, thanks, Bongo.

Cecil I hope you attend some lectures and don't spend all your time in The Eagle like I did!

Philip I do try!

Michael Lonsdale is still there, Dad. Teaching tort.

Cecil Good God, he must be a hundred, if he's a day.

Philip He literally sleeps through every supervision!

The men all laugh. Cecil raises his glass of wine.

Cecil Floreat antiqua domus!

Michael Hear, hear.

Philip Rah, rah, rah! . . . Any interesting cases lately, Dad?

Michael Funnily enough, I was asked to represent the Rolling Stones last week.

Cecil The rock and roll band?

Michael I'm surprised you've heard of them.

Philip Come on, Dad! Everyone's heard of them!

Carol They're Nigel's favourite band –

Michael I said no of course.

Cecil Whatever for?

Michael It's a case made of straw.

Cecil Notwithstanding, it would bring so much prestige for your Chambers.

Philip Everyone will want to represent them, won't they?

Carol (*pointedly*) Yes! And they're Nigel's favourite band!

Michael Huh.

Carol sits for a moment.

Cecil Carol darling, did I ever tell you the time when I was in Newcastle on the Judges' Circuit, and I invited the Beatles round to my chambers for tea?

Carol Yes, Bongo. But I do love that story.

Cecil I made them all give me their autographs. Then I sold them on for a pound apiece!

Cecil, Carol and Philip laugh.

Michael Totally unethical behaviour.

Cecil Rubbish! Very nice boys too. They took a real shine to me.

Carol gets up again.

Carol Nigel! Lunch is ready!

Cecil But the Rolling Stones! I mean! This will be the trial of the decade! My goodness, of course you must represent them, Michael! You must represent them, and you must win!

Nigel enters. He is wearing the outfit that Marianne picked out for him at the shop. His hair is styled. He is wearing make-up. Nigel goes and takes his place at the table, next to his brother.

Philip (*amused*) Christ, Jelly! What have you come as?

Philip ruffles his hair, laughing.

Nigel Don't touch the hair!

Philip Crikey I've only been away a term and you've gone completely off the rails.

Cecil Hello, Nigel.

Carol ignores it.

Carol Do you want a spot of vino, Jelly?

Nigel Thanks, Mummy.

Cecil (*leans in to Carol*) Is Nigel a pretty boy now, Carol?

Carol (*quietly, smiling*) I don't think so, Bongo. But it wouldn't be a problem if he was, would it?

Cecil No of course not!

Pause.

You know I was mistaken for a queer once. I was holding a tambourine at the time. Did I ever tell you that story?

Nigel I don't think so –

Cecil Oh, it was a hoot! Of course, I was such a beautiful young man – ravishing. Wait a minute, I know what you are, Nigel, you're a flower person, aren't you? Excellent! Personally, I rather like those hippy-dippies.

Nigel Thanks, Bongo.

Suddenly Michael raps his fist on the table. They all look at him.

Michael Take it off!

Nigel Take what off?

Michael You know what I'm talking about.

Carol Oh Michael, leave him. He's not hurting anyone.

Michael (*to Nigel*) And wash your face. You will not wear women's lipstick to Sunday lunch. Not in my house.

Nigel What's wrong with women's lipstick?

Cecil I've worn it myself on the odd occasion.

Carol He's just expressing himself!

Michael He can find somewhere else to express himself then . . . And first thing Monday we're cutting that hair.

Nigel You can talk! You wear that stupid shitty wig every day!

Michael Go to your room! Now!

Cecil (*quietly*) Oh dear oh dear oh dear.

Nigel exits.

Carol Well, that's lunch ruined. After I made all that effort.

Pause.

Go and check on him, will you, Philip?

Philip Do I have to?

Carol Yes, and be nice!

Philip exits. Carol pours herself more wine.

That was a total overreaction, Michael! What century were you born in? He's young – he's trying to find himself. You have to give him a little space.

Cecil I'm afraid Carol is right.

Michael It's ever since he's fallen in with that theatre lot.

Carol Oh, what rot.

Cecil Personally, I thought he looked quite nice.

Michael You're as bad as he is!

Cecil The thing about you, Michael, and I mean this in the nicest possible way: you don't understand these things because you were never young.

Michael Nonsense. Of course I was young.

Cecil No, I'm afraid not. I, on the other hand, was young for the longest time.

Michael Oh, shut up, Bongo! Of course I was young –

Cecil I was such a charmer, Carol – I broke so many hearts –

Carol Oh, I believe it!

Michael I broke hearts too! For God's sake, Carol, back me up here. I was young, wasn't I? Carol? Was I young – when I was young? Carol!

Carol You were certainly – younger.

Cecil No, you weren't. Never. You were always a stuffed shirt! Your mother used to say you were the only forty-year-old baby the hospital had ever seen!

Pause.

Come to think of it, you're completely the wrong person to take on the Stones case. They should have asked me.

Michael This is bullying. You are now bullying me.

Carol Oh Michael, we're only joking.

Cecil The thing is, these things do happen, Michael. Between a father and a son.

Michael What are you talking about?

Cecil You were exactly the same.

Michael Rubbish! I was the best sort of son.

Cecil You had your moments.

Michael That's simply not true.

Cecil I will be the judge of that!

Michael How would you even know? You were never there.

Cecil (*prickly*) Well I was on the circuit, building my career. Paying for your very expensive education.

Carol Oh, for heaven's sake, stop it you two. You know – you lawyers – you hate to break with precedent. But sometimes, for the sake of the rest of us, maybe you should. Bongo, go upstairs for your nap –

Cecil Yes, very good. Thank you, Carol dear.

He goes to go. Turns back.

Michael. All I'm saying is – perhaps you ought to let Nigel make his own mistakes. At least then he won't lay the blame at your door.

Carol starts to clear up.

Michael He worshipped me when he was young. I could do no wrong.

Carol Bongo?

Michael No, no, no. Nigel. Now we don't see eye to eye on anything.

Carol You have to cut him some slack.

She passes him a cloth for the washing-up.

Here. Your penance.

Michael (*brooding*) I don't know what Pater was talking about. Pass me the pinny, would you? Of course I was young! I was *young*. I'm still young.

He ties up the pinny.

I'm in the prime of my life.

She is trying not to laugh.

Carol Oh, Michael.

She goes to him.

You know you're still a very attractive man.

Michael Am I?

Carol You are to me . . . Do you remember when we were first married? You always imposed a rumpy-pumpy ban the night before you had a big trial. Then after the verdict you couldn't keep your hands off me. Remember?

Michael Are you sure that was me?

Carol Who else would it be? You were very vigorous in those days.

She touches him.

Michael What are you doing, woman? For God's sake. There's a time and a place.

She recoils from him.

Carol Is there, Michael? Is there? Because I'm not sure there is any more.

Michael What?

She goes back to the table, drains a glass of wine.

I don't know what you're talking about.

Carol The world is changing, Michael! Get with it! Seriously. Or you'll be left behind.

She leaves. He stands there, thinking. After a moment he goes to the phone. He dials.

Michael Clerk's Residence, please . . . Ah, Stan, it's Michael – sorry to disturb you on a Sunday. But it's about that Rolling Stones case. Perhaps we can schedule a meeting?

SCENE SEVEN

Chamber reception/Michael's office.
  The secretaries are in the typing pool. Daphne is overseeing them. One of them looks through the window.

Sheila They're here! The Stones! Oh my flippin' fanny! They're here!

The other secretaries run to the window. Vivek joins them.

Frieda It's Mick!

Sheila And Marianne! Look at her! She's sooooo pretty!

Frieda Oh my God, it's Keith!

Sheila Keith! Keith!

Frieda starts to scream. Sheila joins in.

Daphne Ladies! Stop this at once!

Frieda I can't breathe, Sheila! I can't breathe!

Frieda hyperventilates and faints.

Sheila (*shrieks*) Oh my God, is she dead?

Daphne Of course she's not dead! Oh, goodness me! Get her out of the way before they arrive. Mr Chakrabarti – if you could assist.

Vivek grabs Frieda by the feet and starts to drag her across the floor as the Rolling Stones entourage enter.

Allen is with them. Keith watches the body being dragged away with interest.

(*Stern.*) Good day to you, gentlemen – and –

She looks at Marianne a moment, instinctively disapproves of her.

Mr Havers is expecting you.

She leads them to Michael's office. Michael is there. He shakes their hands.

Michael Mr Klein. Mr Richards. Mr Jagger. Miss –

Marianne Faithfull. As in full of faith.

He takes her hand. He can't help being a little taken with Marianne.

Michael How charming . . . I must say, you look very – familiar.

Marianne Everyone says that to me. They think they know me. But it's just because I'm famous.

Michael I see.

Vivek joins them, having disposed of Frieda.

Vivek Sorry about that!

Mick Don't worry, love. We're used to it.

Michael Welcome all, please take a seat.

Daphne Can I offer you tea or coffee?

Keith You know what, darlin'? I'd love a Scotch.

Daphne (*scandalised*) It's eleven o'clock in the morning!

Michael I'm sure we can rustle something up, Daphne.

Daphne We don't keep alcohol on the premises.

Michael Don't we have some quaffing wine in the cellar?

Daphne It's only for special occasions.

Michael Mr Chakrabarti, see what you can do for us, will you?

Vivek Yes of course.

He gets up and leaves the office, accompanied by a disgruntled Daphne.

Michael So, your case will be heard at the West Sussex Quarter Session in June –

Marianne The pills were mine!

Michael I beg your pardon?

Mick Babe! You don't have to say that!

Marianne I don't care. I can take it.

Keith She can take it, Mike, trust me.

Marianne The pills they found on Mick. They were really mine all along . . . I want you to bring the full force of the Law down on me.

Michael Is this true?

Mick They were both of ours –

Marianne I'm not afraid to speak up. I want my day in court! I'll give them what for!

Allen Yeah, I don't think that's a good idea, Marianne – you know how you can get –

Marianne No. How can I get, Allen?

Allen You – you're emotional.

Marianne I'm not.

Mick You are, babe.

Keith Yeah, you are.

Marianne But I'm just trying to protect you all –

Allen No need, is there, Mr Havers?

Allen shakes his head almost imperceptibly at Michael.

Michael No, no. And anyway, I wouldn't dream of putting a young lady on the stand.

Marianne But that's not fair – I was there –

Allen Good call, Havers. That's settled then!

Marianne reacts.

Michael We don't yet know which judge has been assigned –

Marianne (*interrupting*) Can I smoke?

Michael swallows his dislike of this.

Michael Ermm. Yes. Of course.

He takes an ashtray from his desk drawer and gives it to her.

Allen The main thing is you gotta keep my boys out of prison –

Michael Don't worry, Mr Klein, nobody's going to prison.

Keith Thank fuck for that!

Michael stares at Keith.

Michael (*sternly*) That sort of language won't serve you in the courtroom, Mr Richards.

Marianne starts to roll a cigarette.

Allen The boys will be on their best behaviour, I'll make sure of that. Mick here went to Oxford University you know.

Michael Really?! Cambridge man myself –

Mick (*RP*) You've got it all wrong. I went to the London School of Economics. I quit after a year, alas.

Michael Still. A university man. That should play in our favour . . . You speak very nicely too, Mr Jagger, when you wish to.

Mick Thank you.

Michael See that you stick to that nice BBC English. No straying into that mock cockney all you young people like. The jury will prefer that. Yes?

Marianne I speak nicely too.

Michael You certainly do.

Marianne My mother is an Austrian baroness. I am descended from the von Sacher-Masochs of Vienna –

Michael (*falling under her spell*) Are you really?

Allen But we've already established that Miss Faithfull won't be testifying.

Michael Quite. Which leaves you, Mr Richards –

Keith I went to Dartford Technical College. Any good for you?

Michael Well –

Keith I grew up on a council estate. Oh and I'm an anarchist –

Michael Best not mention that.

Michael is again distracted by Marianne who is crumbling hash into her cigarette.

Michael I'm sorry – excuse me, miss – that's not Indian hemp, is it?

Marianne Do you want a puff? It will open the doors of your mind!

Allen Marianne?! What the – ?

Marianne Don't get heavy. It's just a joke.

Michael (*to Marianne*) May I remind you, young lady that we are under the jurisdiction of her Majesty the Queen here!

Marianne (*curtsying*) So sorry, Your Majesty.

Marianne, Mick and Keith start to laugh.

Michael Oh, I see what this is! You are making a mockery of me. I think we'd better call a halt to this right now, don't you?

Allen No, no, Mike. That's not – I know what you're thinking but that's a – Turkish cigarette –

Mick Yeah, we got it in Turkey!

Marianne Constantinople.

Keith Totally Turkish, Mike. Cross my heart and hope to die.

Allen They're completely off the hard stuff. I give you my word. Marianne! For Christ's sake!

Marianne All right!

Sulkily she puts the unlit reefer back in the tin. She closes it. She absently puts the tin on the chair.

Michael Perhaps it would be better if the young lady were to take a seat outside?

Allen Marianne – go wait outside.

Marianne But I don't want to –

Mick It's all right, babe. I don't want you getting all worked up.

Keith Off you pop, Marianne. We can handle this.

After a reluctant pause, Marianne leaves.

SCENE EIGHT

Chambers.
Nigel runs on stage.

Nigel (*to the audience*) So Mum told me that they're in there today. Seeing Dad. The real live actual Stones! I mean this is an important cultural moment in my life. I couldn't miss this opportunity, could I?

Vivek runs on with a bottle of Scotch.

Hey, Vivek!

Vivek Hello there, Nigel! What brings you here? I'm afraid your father is rather busy at the moment –

Nigel It wasn't him I wanted to see. Are Mick Jagger and Keith Richards still here?

Vivek Ah-ha! On the hunt for an autograph, are you? Want to meet Mick and Keith in person? I don't blame you. They really do have something about them . . . Mind you, that Richards fellow is a little grubby. Mick on the other hand has a raw animal magnetism. I look at him and all I see is golden light.

Nigel Can I come in then?

Vivek I'll smuggle you in!

Nigel Yes please!

Suddenly Nigel sees Marianne appear.

Oh wait a minute! Marianne! I mean Miss Faithfull.

Vivek Are you coming then?

Nigel Don't worry, Vivek. Maybe later.

Nigel is staring at Marianne. Vivek takes this in.

Vivek Ah. I see where the river flows. Very good. Goodbye, Nigel.

Vivek runs off with his whisky.

Marianne Are you following me?

Nigel No. Yes. Sort of. The reason I'm here is my dad is –

Marianne Havers, Nigel Havers! That stuck-up lawyer is your dad?

Nigel Yes. But I mean we're totally different. Totally.

Marianne They've just kicked me out! The bloody cheek of it! Anyway, I don't care. The whole thing's a gas . . . So. You're a fan of the Stones then?

Nigel Of course!

Marianne Why do you like them?

Nigel They're the greatest rock band in the world.

Marianne Yes, I suppose they are.

Nigel But I mean I'm more of a fan of you – obviously –

Marianne You don't have to say that.

Nigel I thought you were wonderful in the play –

Marianne Oh. that's all over. I've had to take a break. My nerves.

Nigel I'm sorry.

Marianne It's fine! The money in theatre is terrible anyway. I've got plenty of other things to do.

Marianne looks at her watch.

Shit.

Nigel What?

Marianne I forgot. I've got a gig. Work.

She looks at him.

You'd better come with me then.

Nigel What? No, I couldn't – I mean if it's work –

Marianne Got anything better to do?

Nigel Erm –

Nigel turns to the audience.

(*To the audience.*) Do I have anything better to do than to accompany the most beautiful girl in the world to wherever she wants to go?

Marianne Havers!

Nigel (*to the audience*) I don't think so.

Marianne Come on then, choppity-chop.

She leads him off.

SCENE NINE

Chambers, Michael's office.
 Vivek has now joined the others. The Stones and Allen drink Scotch.

Allen What we're saying, Mr Havers, is that it was all a set-up. Redlands. The raid. They planned it – tell him, Mick.

Mick Yeah right, so at the beginning of February the *News of the World* printed a story claiming I'd admitted to taking LSD. Which I hadn't. It was all bullshit.

Keith They mistook him for Brian, the idiots.

Michael Brian?

Vivek Brian Jones. I believe he's in the band.

Mick You think we're bad –

Keith Brian is a loose cannon.

Michael makes a note.

Mick So I issued the *News of the World* with a writ. I'm not having them piss me about like that. I'm suing the paper for defamation.

Allen We're talking damages running into six figures.

Vivek Oh my goodness!

Mick They can't go tellin' lies about me like that. Trying to ruin my reputation.

Vivek Charlatans.

Mick Exactly.

Michael (*interested*) So what you're saying is, you think the *News of the World* were looking for an opportunity to shame you publicly?

Keith Yeah for sure – this was a sting – to entrap them –

Mick The police raid happened only five days after I accused them of libel. It's bleedin' obvious! They wanted to get back at me. So they had something to defend themselves with in court. Prove I was a naughty boy, so that they wouldn't have to pay out to me.

Michael Good God. Let me get this straight? You believe the *News of the World* were working in cahoots with the police in order to frame you?

Keith What else?

Mick They think we're getting a bit too big for our boots so they want to put us in our place.

Allen I wouldn't be surprised if MI5 was involved. This goes high, believe me. Straight to the top.

   Pause.

Michael But that's preposterous –

Allen It's just not British, huh?

Michael (*indicating the Scotch*) Pour me some of that, will you, Vivek?

Vivek pours him a Scotch.

Mick We need to expose them all. The *News of the World*. The police. Right? They can't do that, can they? Just because we're famous.

Keith We're being punished for being young and hip.

Allen It's just not right.

Vivek No.

Michael Hmmm.

Michael gets up and paces a little.

The problem is an agent provocateur defence can be extremely risky. The Sussex Police Constabulary and the *News of the World* are not on trial here. We would need cast-iron proof that they acted illegally. Do you know who tipped off the police? The actual person –

Mick The journalist who wrote the piece is Derek Carter –

Keith Fuckin' arsewipe . . . Well he is!

Allen Presumably Carter or the editor got in touch with Scotland Yard –

Michael Scotland Yard? You think this went as far as Scotland Yard? Do you have proof?

Allen The proof is we're sitting here with you. You think West Sussex Constabulary give a shit what Keith does in his own home? Nah – this came from higher up. The powers that be, they want to stop my boys getting any more famous.

Pause.

Michael Mmm. As shocking as it is, personally I think this is a dangerous route to go down. It might alienate the jury.

Allen How so?

Michael People don't like their beloved national institutions being called into question. It destabilises them. This is Chichester we're talking about, after all. I think we should proceed cautiously –

Allen Are you sure about that? This is corruption on a major scale –

Michael The aim is to keep the band out of prison, yes? So they can go on performing?

Mick All we care about is the fans.

Keith And the music –

Mick Bringing the music to the fans, yeah!

Michael If that's the case then I think we should tread a more conservative path.

Allen Really?

Michael These are minor offences after all. You must have faith in the English Law, gentlemen. Don't worry, this case is going to be very straightforward. I fully expect you both to get off with a sharp rap on the knuckles.

Allen Well. You know best.

Vivek Oh he does!

Michael I do. Good. I think that's all I need for now. I don't want to waste any more of your precious time. I'll see you in court, gentlemen.

They stand up. Keith goes to hug him – a level of physical intimacy that Michael is not at all comfortable with.

Keith Nice work. Come here, big man –

Michael (*flustered*) No no no thank you.

Keith Okay. That's the way you want it.

Mick (*handing Vivek his glass*) Thanks, mate.

Vivek Vivek. Please call me Vivek.

Mick Vivek.

Allen shakes Michael's hand.

Allen Just remember, Mikey – I'm putting the future of the Rolling Stones in your hands. Yeah?

Michael Of course. The Stones will be rolling in no time.

They all look at him.

Vivek, show them out, would you?

They leave. Michael sighs and drinks some Scotch. He extemporises a little.

Gentlemen of the jury, you see before you two fine, upstanding young men –

Pause.

Two artists of considerable status in the world of 'pop'. Ugh.

He notices the tin of tobacco on one of the chairs. He picks it up and looks at it.

Ugh.

SCENE TEN

Studio.
A photography studio in East London. Marianne enters wearing a dressing gown, followed by Nigel. Terry, a macho photographer in his twenties, appears, camera in hand.

Marianne I'm sorry I'm late, Terry. I had to see my lawyer.

Terry In trouble again?

Marianne You know me.

Terry Naughty girl. What we gonna do about you, eh, Marianne? Good job you're such a looker. Hey. What's this? Who's the kid?

Marianne looks at Nigel.

Marianne My little brother.

Nigel (*to the audience*) BROTHER? . . . LITTLE?

Terry You're full of surprises.

Marianne It's all right if he stays, isn't it?

Terry He's not going to cramp your style?

Marianne I like having him around. He relaxes me.

Terry All right then. So long as he doesn't get in the way.

Terry is setting up some lighting for the shoot.

You get yourself ready, darlin'.

Marianne takes off her dressing gown. Underneath she is wearing a black basque and suspenders or something similarly revealing.

Marianne (*to Nigel*) Don't look at me.

Nigel (*looking at her, then looking away*) No, I'm not, sorry.

Marianne Oh all right. Just a peek . . . You know this isn't me, right? I prefer a high neck! I'm practically Victorian when left to my own devices. But my manager says I haven't had a hit for ages.

Nigel But if you're uncomfortable like this – you could say no –

Marianne That's really not how it works, Nigel. You wouldn't understand.

Nigel Sorry.

Pause.

What does Mick say? Does he mind?

Marianne Oh Mick! Everyone thinks that Mick must be a maniac – you know – in bed and everything. But he's actually very soft and cuddly. When we're at home together, you'd hardly recognise him. He looks after me. It's just, well, lately, he's preoccupied with the court case.

Pause.

I don't mind anyway. It's all just a ride!

Pause.

You know I wasn't looking for all this. I got discovered at a party. I was just minding my own business and this promoter saw me. He said to me I had a face that could sell records.

Pause.

He didn't even know if I could sing – he didn't care.

Nigel But you can sing!

Marianne Yes, I can. I know I'm not like Mick. But I've got my own flavour. I've got something to offer, I know that.

Nigel Absolutely.

Marianne I want to write more of my own stuff. I have things I want to say. Different to what they think.

Pause.

Nigel I think you're amazing.

Marianne Hey, Havers, you know what? I like you.

Nigel I like you too. But not in that way. I mean –

Terry Marianne!

Marianne Coming!

She looks at Nigel

This is for the public. I've got to do something to make them love me, haven't I?

She moves off towards the set.

Nigel (*to the audience*) This is all terribly confusing.

Nigel sits cross-legged on the floor. She starts to pose for the camera.

Terry Come on then, girl. Let's give them all something to look at . . . I want you sexy – but innocent at the same time. Can you do that for me? That's it. Oh and hands through the hair. Crackin'. Open your mouth a bit. Lean forward. Lovely.

Marianne sings 'This Little Bird' by John D. Loudermilk. As she sings, Marianne poses for Terry.

That's it, babe. Think I've got all I need.

Nigel joins in for the second verse and chorus. This is a moment of connection for them.

SCENE ELEVEN

White Shutters.

Michael is in his pyjamas, reading the News of the World. *Carol enters in her conservative nightwear, her hair in rollers.*

Carol I meant to tell you I had a phone call from the school today.

Michael (*shaking his head*) Unbelievable. Listen to this. 'Miss X was wrapped in a fur rug, and she was not wearing any underwear –' Miss X is Marianne Faithfull by the way. And the inference is she had a Mars bar in her – you know what –

Carol No. What?

Michael In her – erm –

Pause.

In her voovar –

Carol Her voovar?

Michael Yes, you know . . . Her lady-fortress – 'down below'.

Carol You mean her vagina?

Michael Carol!

Carol Michael, I love you but you really are a stuffed shirt.

He harrumphs and looks back at the paper.

Anyway, the headmaster rang – about Nigel –

Michael (*not listening*) Oh Good God! Apparently, she inserted the confectionery – and Mr Jagger was – there's no polite way of putting this, I'm afraid, Carol – he was licking it. With a view to eating it.

Carol Oh! How very creative!

Michael Jagger says it's not true. Mind you, having met the girl myself I wouldn't be so sure.

Carol I take it the case has finally caught your imagination?

Michael She wanted to testify – Miss X – but she's clearly a loose cannon. It's bad enough having to represent the boys.

Carol So, you are going to represent them?

Michael I might as well. It's hardly a taxing case.

Carol Well just so you know, there's someone else you need to represent –

Michael Who?

Carol Nigel. I've been trying to tell you. He's in trouble at school.

Michael What now?

Carol I don't want you to get angry – but apparently, he's been bunking off –

Michael What?

Carol It's happened a few times – I'm worried about him.

Michael Does he know how much I am paying for his education?

Carol He needs our support –

Michael He has important exams next summer –

Carol I don't think he's happy at school –

Michael I'm not having this. You'll have to talk some sense into him –

Carol Me? Why is it always me?

Michael I talked to him already. And what good did it do? Besides I haven't got time for this. I'm about to go into a major trial.

Carol And that's more important than your own son?

Michael He does it on purpose to rile me –

Carol He doesn't – don't be ridiculous –

Michael gets up.

Where are you going?

Michael To do some work. The Rolling Stones are a major contemporary rock ensemble, Carol. Their future is at stake.

He exits. Carol is left exasperated.

Carol Gordon Bennett!

She picks up the paper and throws it into the wastepaper basket.

SCENE TWELVE

Chichester Crown Court.
 A crowd of fans wait for a glimpse of their pop idols. There is a T-shirt seller hawking his wares. He 'wears' a small tray with sweets, etc., like a theatre usher. There is also a police presence.

Male Usher Get your Redlands memorabilia! T-shirts, mugs, key rings!

A Female News Reporter comes on, speaking into a microphone.

Female News Reporter (*very BBC, starchy*) It's an ordinary summer's day in the respectable market town of Chichester. Hitherto it has been primarily famous for its towering cathedral, symbolic of its authority as the capital of West

Sussex. The local economy is based on agriculture – and its citizens are, on the whole, conservative, law-abiding people. That is why it is such an extraordinary day here at Chichester Crown Court where the biggest celebrity trial this town has ever seen is about to take place. The rock group – the Rolling Stones –

The fans scream.

That is to say, two members of the Rolling Stones –

The fans scream.

Mick Jagger –

The fans scream.

and Keith Richards –

The fans scream. The News Reporter turns to the crowd.

Yes, all right, we get the picture!

She collects herself.

The aforementioned face serious drugs charges today and I can say with absolute certainty that Chichester, or Chi as it is known affectionately, has never seen the like. The temperature is set to rise today both inside and outside the court.

Michael sweeps in in his barrister finery, with Vivek as his junior counsel. From the other side of the stage Allen enters.

Allen So, gents, are we all set?

Michael As ready as we'll ever be. The boys are in good form?

Allen Never better.

Michael No funny business?

Allen Pinky promise.

Michael Hmmm . . . I didn't think it would attract such a crowd.

Allen My boys are famous.

Michael Well they may be famous out here but it won't make a jot of difference inside the court. Let's go in then, shall we?

Allen So how long will this take do you think?

Michael Oh not long, couple of days, with a fair wind.

Female News Reporter (*into microphone*) And that is Michael Havers, the Counsel for Defence, with his team. And I believe the man wearing a wig is, yes, that's Allen Klein, the manager of the Rolling Stones.

Allen (*shouts behind him*) Hey, lady! This is not a wig!

Female News Reporter (*into microphone*) Correction. That is his own hair. And yes, they're going in! They're entering the court for the Trial of the Century.

Lights change. They enter the courtroom.
Allen, Michael and Vivek take their places.

Allen Hey, Mikey, I don't know why but I feel nervous.

Michael No need for that.

Vivek Rest assured, Mr Klein! You are being represented by the very best! Just you wait!

Clerk Gentlemen of the jury!

The jury 'arrive'. This is the audience. They all look at them.

Allen Christ. Is that the jury? They look pretty hostile.

Michael Good Sussex farm folk. Nothing wrong with that.

Allen They may as well have come with their shovels.

Michael Now, now. We must show the utmost respect towards our jury.

Allen Looks like some of them would rather not be here.

Michael Oh they're always like that.

Vivek I say! Have they allowed a woman onto the jury?

Allen No way!

Michael God forbid!

They all stare.

The lighting isn't good but I'm pretty sure that's a man.

They turn away from the audience.

Allen What about the judge? Is he a fan of rock?

Michael Unfortunately, we've been a little unlucky there.

Clerk All rise for the Honourable Lord Justice Leslie Block.

The court rises. Judge Block enters. He is miserable-looking, fifties/sixties.

Allen Christ. He looks like an executioner.

Vivek Funny you should say that.

Michael They call him the Hanging Judge.

Block Be seated.

Michael He's old-school but he's very experienced.

They all sit.

Block Bring in the defendants.

Mick appears first, dressed extravagantly.

Michael Dear God in heaven! Jagger's in fancy dress.

Keith appears next, dressed like a peacock. The fans go wild. Michael can't believe it.

Michael And Richards has come as Beau Brummell. I thought you said they were going to take this seriously.

Allen This is them taking it seriously. They dressed up for you, Mikey!

Fans (*screaming*) Mick! Keith!

Female Fan I love you, Keith.

Mick and Keith blow kisses and wave to the fans.

Michael Tell them to stop that! They're not supposed to be enjoying it.

Fan Justice for Mick and Keith!

Allen YEAH! JUSTICE FOR MY BOYS!

Michael Mr Klein!

Female Fan MARRY ME, Keith!

Block Order in court!

Michael You said the fans were going to behave themselves.

Allen Oh the fans are feral. Ain't nothing I can do about that.

Michael But it's going to seriously prejudice the jury.

Pause.

I've made a terrible mistake. I should have followed my first instincts –

Allen The press are all over this, Havers. You've gotta save my boys. Or you'll be the laughing stock.

Michael This is going to be the end of my career!

Block Counsel for the Defence!

Clerk Michael Havers QC.

Slowly Michael gathers himself and stands up.

Michael Your Honour, the defendants have been charged with the possession of – amphetamine sulphate and methyl amphetamine hydrochloride . . . Yes. And I need not remind you, gentlemen of the jury, that under the Law we are all presumed innocent till proved guilty. I am going to put to you that on the night in question, my clients were enjoying a polite gathering in the private home of Mr Keith Richards. Redlands. A sizeable Tudor mansion in the quiet oasis of West Wittering. West Wittering for goodness' sake! . . . I will further prove to you that in Redlands on the night in question, no laws were broken, no by-laws infringed, police intervention was in fact entirely unnecessary. This, gentlemen of the jury, is what we Englishmen call a storm in a teacup.

He turns to Mick and Keith.

Look at them. What do you see? Underneath the, erm – clothes and also the – demeanour . . . I will tell you what I see:

Pause.

Two sweet, innocent young men!

Mick That's right!

Keith It's a set-up!

Mick We've been framed.

Keith It's a load of bollocks. Crusty old bastards!

Mick None of this is even real!

Block (*pounding his gavel*) The defendants will be silent!

Michael Yes, Your Honour.

Mick 'Fraid not! No can do.

Keith Our future is at stake!

Mick We will not be silenced.

Keith Hand me my guitar, would you?

Mick Listen to the fans! They know the truth!

Fans Yeah!!

Someone hands Keith a guitar.
Music starts: 'Can I Get a Witness' by Holland, Dozier, Holland. Mick, Keith and ensemble start to rock out.

Block Order! Order!

Mick sings the song. Keith sings backing lyrics. The Fans go wild and start to dance. Everyone is dancing soon, including Vivek.
Music cuts suddenly. Spot on a bewildered Michael.

Michael This is not a trial, it's a pantomime!

Block You must control your clients, Havers. I will not have this! Clear the court.

Michael goes and gathers up his brief.

Michael Mr Chakrabarti? Are you coming?

Vivek I'll – I'll be right with you, sir.

Michael Oh that's the way it's going to be, is it?

Michael takes one last look at the court:

God help me!

He storms out. The music starts up again. Vivek dances wildly. Mick and Keith sing the remainder of the song, backed by the ensemble.
End of Act One.

Act Two

SCENE ONE

Music: 'Soul Limbo', theme tune to Test Match Special.
We are at Lord's for a Test match.
Through the scene we hear the gentle sounds of ball on bat and crowd response at intervals. The Cricket Commentator walks on stage and talks into an old-fashioned radio mike to the audience.

Cricket Commentator (*very RP*) Well here we are then at Lord's on a lovely sunny afternoon – back for the start of the second innings for England. Bhagwath Chandrasekhar is bowling the first ball of the innings to John Edrich.

The sound of bat on ball.

Well, he's hit that one hard, yes and that's a six into the Mound stand! A good hook that off a short ball. Edrich gets off the mark with a vengeance!

The crowd applaud. We are in the MCC stand with Nigel and Cecil. Cecil is wearing his MCC jacket and tie. Nigel is in his school uniform but no tie, collar up, mussed-up hair.

Cecil Shot! Well played.

Nigel Come on, England!
(*To the audience.*) Love cricket. It's a me and Bongo thing.

They watch the cricket.

Cecil I wonder how your father's getting on.

Nigel (*bitterly*) He'll win, won't he? He always wins.

Cecil looks at Nigel.

Cecil You two still not getting on?

Nigel shrugs.

Have you ever seen him in action? In court I mean.

Nigel No.

Cecil Oh! You should go along. Watch him! You might enjoy it.

Nigel I don't think so.

Cecil He's a real showman when he wants to be. I think you'd appreciate it.

Nigel I'd rather not.

Pause.

Cecil He thinks the world of you, you know.

Nigel He's got a funny way of showing it.

Cecil Yes, well, that's our way in this family.

Pause.

You know I've been thinking about your father. And he hasn't always been like he is now. He was actually a rather sensitive little chap. When he was a boy. He'd cry at the passing of a fly. Honestly. I found it rather irritating.

Pause.

What I'm saying is – your father's had to work terribly hard to become the man that he is. But underneath all that he's rather . . . I was perhaps a little hard on him when he was younger . . . Not that I would say any of that to him, of course.

Pause.

Here. I've got something to cheer you up.

Nigel What?

He reaches in his pocket and brings out an MCC tie. Hands it to Nigel.

Cecil Congratulations! You are now a member of the MCC!

Nigel Seriously? But I thought there was a massive waiting list –

Cecil (*tapping his nose*) It's not what you know. It's *who* you know.

Nigel Thanks, Bongo!

He hugs his grandfather.

Cecil Glad to have you as part of the club, my boy.

Nigel puts the tie on during the next.

Nigel (*quietly*) The thing is, Bongo I don't think I want to be a lawyer. I want to be an actor –

Cecil (*looking at the action*) Stupid bloody bugger!

Nigel What?

Cricket Commentator Yes, he's edged it, diving catch at second slip by Pataudi.

Cecil He's out! Did you see that? Utterly reckless.

Nigel Did you hear me, Bongo?

Cecil (*to the retreating batsman*) You should be ashamed of yourself!

Nigel What?

Cecil Barrington out for a duck!

Nigel Oh. Yes.

Cecil What did you say?

Nigel Nothing.

Cecil D'Oliviera's in next. He'll show them what he's made of. Eh?

Nigel (*lacklustre*) Yes.

Cecil glances at Nigel.

Cecil (*watching the crease*) No need to be down in the dumps, my boy. I'm here for you. Whatever you decide . . . But the sad fact is your father can be terribly stubborn. My advice to you is to cut him some slack. Maybe try and meet him halfway. There's a good chap.

Cecil pats his grandson on the knee. Then he looks back at the action.

Oh, bugger me! He's been clean bowled. Out for a golden duck. Oh Dolly, Dolly, Dolly!

Cricket Commentator We interrupt the cricket to bring you news of extraordinary scenes at Chichester Crown Court. Excitement is building today as both Mick Jagger and Keith Richards will be called upon to testify. But the question remains: will the rock and roll duo be able to win over the hearts and minds of the jury?

Cecil exits. Nigel remains on stage. He watches the following.

SCENE TWO

Courtroom.
 Music: Mick and Keith grab their microphones and sing: 'Mercy, Mercy' by Don Covay and Ronald Alonzo Miller. The ensemble provides backing vocals.
 Michael is there. He interjects between verses.

Michael Gentlemen of the jury, I want you to look at these two young men. But I want you to remember that first impressions can be misleading. You may think you know who these young men are, but you do not.

They sing.

There is really no need to be scared of them. I want you to look at them as if they were your own sons. Above all remember, that today in this venerable court of law we are all on a level playing field.

They sing. Michael returns to his seat, smug after his performance. Nigel looks at him and turns to the audience.

Nigel (*to the audience*) Would you please stop encouraging him? All right, all right, I know he's good. But he's so annoying. Look, it's not that I don't want him to win. Obviously, I'd like the Stones to be victorious. It's just that he always expects to win. And I hate that. Sometimes I think it would be good for him to lose. Just once. Anyway, I've got to go now because I'm not actually in this bit. Don't worry, I'll be back . . . I must confess I am not strictly observing the theatrical unities of time and place. Sorry about that.

A disgruntled Nigel leaves the stage. The Clerk stands.

Clerk Call to the stand Inspector Gordon Bramley –

Bramley appears in the stand. Michael stands again.

Michael You were the officer in charge of the raid on Redlands, correct?

Bramley That is correct.

Michael So, on the night in question, you and your men surrounded Redlands. But as I understand it only after you heard that George Harrison had left the party? Why was that?

Bramley No reason that I know of. It was just a matter of timings.

Michael I would suggest that you waited till George Harrison left because you weren't after the Beatles. It was the Stones you wanted. This was a targeted attack, wasn't it?

Bramley I wouldn't say so –

Michael (*interrupting*) So then you entered the premises. Did you have to break the door down?

Bramley No, we didn't.

Michael NO! In fact, you were welcomed in by the defendants, weren't you?

Bramley Well. They opened the door to us.

Michael They did not resist you in anyway?

Bramley We had a warrant –

Michael But they let you in without complaint. As I understand it, they encouraged you to warm yourselves by the fire.

Bramley I suppose so.

Michael Yes. They were most accommodating. Then you proceeded to ransack the house, causing hundreds of pounds' worth of damage. Correct?

Bramley We had a job to do.

Michael Which you did with excessive force. During the raid did my clients co-operate with you? They did, didn't they? They behaved in a thoroughly adult manner.

Bramley Well, I wouldn't say –

Michael (*interrupting him*) They readily submitted to full body searches, did they not?

Bramley They did.

Michael Yes. They were polite and courteous at all times. I believe Mr Richards even offered to make you a pot of Earl Grey tea –

Bramley I don't drink tea –

Michael But the point is they behaved as if they were not worried that you would find anything incriminating –

Bramley But we did!

Michael Yes. Let's speak to that. Four tablets of Benzedrine –

A spotlight comes up on Mick.

How did it come about that you had four tablets of Benzedrine in your jacket pocket, Mr Jagger?

Mick (*RP*) I was taking them – for stress.

Michael So, what you are saying is that you had these pills on prescription from a doctor?

Mick I have been prescribed them previously by my doctor, yes. On more than one occasion. But these actual pills I picked up in Italy when we were on tour.

Michael As I understand it you can purchase these tablets quite legally in Italy? Over the counter, yes?

Mick That's right. But I still spoke to my doctor in England about taking them – of course – and he okayed it.

Michael So, you purchased the tablets legally. And to all intents and purposes these were prescribed by a doctor in absentia.

Mick That's correct.

Michael And how do these pills help you?

Mick They keep me going. Performing I mean. I don't know if you've ever seen me on stage, but I like to put on a show. Give the fans what you want.

Michael As I understand it, when you sing, you move in a very energetic fashion?

Mick Oh, very energetic.

Michael Quite. Finally, can I ask you to share your academic record with the jury, Mr Jagger?

Mick (*smiling*) I have seven O levels and two A levels.

Michael turns to the jury.

Michael I think this proves my point that Mr Michael Jagger is in fact a mild-mannered, middle-class man and not the long-haired lout that the *News of the World* would have you believe. Nothing further, Your Honour.

SCENE THREE

Court.
The Male Usher is there, selling snacks and memorabilia. Marianne and Nigel meet outside.

Male Usher Get your T-shirts! Justice for the Redlands Two!

Marianne Havers, Nigel Havers! Fancy meeting you here. Come to see your dad?

Nigel Something like that.

Marianne Good. You can keep me company. I need an ally. Apparently, they're going to be talking about me today.

Nigel But you're not on trial.

Marianne I wish I was. I'd give them what for. But they won't let me. Your dad said he wouldn't put me through it.

Nigel Why not?

Marianne Nobody cares what I have to say. I'm just the little woman. Oh, but they think they can talk *about* me all they want. It's all such nonsense.

Nigel Yes.

Marianne The press has got overexcited because I was wearing a fur rug. I don't know what all the fuss is about. I was cold!

Nigel I mean why else would you wear one?

Marianne They're making me out to be some brainless bimbo.

Male Usher (*holds up a Mars bar*) Fancy a snack?! Have a Mars bar!

Marianne You hear that?!

Nigel Er – yes.

Marianne You know what they said I did?

Nigel I mean, vaguely.

Marianne I would never allow that.

Nigel No!

Marianne So unhygienic. It's just a dirty old man's fantasy. I don't even like Mars bars.

Nigel No, nor me! Hate them. I'm never going to eat another one. In solidarity.

Pause.

Marianne The problem is the press is after me. I mean I don't care what they say about me but imagine what my parents think. It's all so embarrassing. Plus, all the fans already hate me because I stole Mick from them.

Nigel I'm sure that's not what they think.

Marianne Oh, it's absolutely what they think. And worse.

Pause.

Nigel Well hopefully my dad can save the day.

Marianne He's good, is he?

Nigel Oh absolutely. He's the best. In court that is.

Marianne I'm glad I've got you with me. You make me feel a bit braver. Come on then. Let's get this over with.

She exits towards the court.

SCENE THREE B

Lights up on the courtroom.
During the next, Marianne enters, followed by Nigel.

Michael I call to the stand, Constable Rosemary Flint –

Vivek (*discreetly to Michael*) Miss X has arrived.

Michael Ah good, she's dressed like a nun.

Vivek She appears to be with – is that – ?

Michael Nigel?! What the –

He sees Marianne and Nigel arrive and take a seat in the gallery. It puts Michael off his stroke a moment.
Constable Flint enters and takes her place in the witness stand.

Block Your witness is ready, Mr Havers.

Michael nods in Nigel and Marianne's direction and then continues.

Michael Thank you, Your Honour.

He turns to the witness.

So, Constable Flint, let me take you back to the night at Redlands. What were your first impressions when you entered the house?

Flint I knew at once that drugs had been consumed.

Michael And how did you know that, Constable?

Flint There was a very funny smell.

Michael You must have the olfactory powers of a sniffer dog, Miss Flint.

Flint I am in fact known for my smell.

Michael But I can reveal that what you were sensing was actually sandalwood. Sticks of Indian incense were burning inside the house –

Flint I don't know about that. But it smelt queer. And then there was the behaviour of the girl. Marianne –

Michael (*interrupting her*) You are referring of course to Miss X – as we have agreed to call her?

Flint Miss X-rated more like.

Laughter in court.

Block Order! Order!

Michael How was the young lady behaving, Constable Flint?

Flint Salacious, is the word for it.

Michael Can you clarify what you mean by that?

Flint Well for a start she wasn't wearing anything except a rug.

Allen Oh come on!

Michael It was a sizeable rug, wasn't it? Eight foot squared as I understand it. It more than covered her body. Doesn't sound immodest to me.

Flint (*warming to her theme*) Yes, but she kept letting it slip down. And she was completely starkers underneath. In a roomful of men mind you, and she didn't care one bit! In fact, I got the impression she was rather enjoying it.

Rumbles of discontent in the room.

Fan Jezebel!

Allen is shaking his head, sadly. Michael is a little thrown.

Nigel It's not true! None of that is true!

Michael Nigel!

Block Silence in court!

Nigel stands in the gallery.

Nigel Marianne is not on trial! And besides she's not that sort of girl.

Michael Miss X. We are calling her Miss X! And what do you know about it?

Nigel More than you do.

Michael Who invited you anyway?

Nigel Bongo.

Michael Might have known. Trying to sabotage me.

Marianne It's okay, Nigel. Leave it.

Michael (*to Nigel*) Yes! Pipe down!

Block What is this, Mr Havers? Please contain yourself!

Michael Yes, Your Honour. Forgive me.

He turns to the witness.

(*Irritated.*) That will be all, Constable Flint.

Flint leaves the stand. Michael confers privately with Vivek and Allen.

This is not going the way I planned.

Allen You don't say.

Michael You know what I think? The girl in the infernal rug is going to lose it for us.

Allen Why?

Michael She's just too much for the fine folk of Chichester. And I can't say I blame them.

Vivek Don't lose heart, Michael. You can turn this around. I know you can.

Michael You think? I've got the imbecile up next!

Clerk Call to the stand Mr Keith Richards.

Keith appears in the stand.

Keith (*cool*) All right, cockers!

The fans scream.

Block Order! Order!

Clerk Raise your right hand!

Keith (*making a peace sign*) Peace! Peace, man. Peace, yeah?

The fans settle.

Michael Mr Richards. Would you say on the night in question that Miss X's appearance was indecent?

Keith Nah. The thing about Mar— I mean Miss X – is she's a lovely girl but she don't wear much at the best of times.

Pause.

In fact, she was more decent in that rug than I'd seen her in quite a while.

Michael You weren't shocked by her behaviour that evening then?

Keith Not in the least.

Michael Why not?

Keith Because I'm not an old man.

Pause.

Michael What exactly do you mean by that?

Keith What I say. We are young men. And you lot –

Keith looks defiantly at Block. And then the jury. Lastly, he looks at Michael.

You are old men.

Michael looks at Vivek for confirmation. Did he mean me? Vivek is keeping out of it. Michael looks back at Keith.

Yeah you're old. And we just don't wanna live by your petty bourgeois morals no more.

Nigel Hear, hear!

Keith Thanks, mate.

Block Order, order! Move on, Havers.

Michael wipes his face with a handkerchief. He looks at Vivek and Allen.

Michael Mr Richards, there was a man at the party who wasn't invited, I understand.

Keith Yeah, Dave Sniderman.

Michael Did you know him?

Keith I'd met him once. In New York.

Michael And Mr Sniderman has another alias as I understand it?

Keith They call him the Acid King.

There are ripples around the court. Sharp intakes of breath.

Michael Why do they call him that?

Keith Because he's a pusher. He sells drugs to celebrities.

More ripples.

Michael So how did he know about the party?

Keith Beats me. He wasn't invited. He must have been tipped off.

Michael Tipped off?

Keith By the *News of the World*. On account of Mick's lawsuit against them.

Block Supposition. I will not admit that. Strike it from the record.

Allen What? No! You gotta be kidding me?

Pause.

Michael You have been under intense media scrutiny in the last few months, have you not, Mr Richards?

Keith Months?! We haven't had any privacy since 1964.

Michael But this gathering was an attempt – at least – at some 'down time'?

Keith An Englishman's home is his castle, isn't that what they say?

Michael Quite, and I know you carefully selected your home – Redlands – a fifteenth-century baronial dwelling –

Keith With a moat!

Michael With a moat no less – you bought Redlands in the quiet seaside village of West Wittering in order to find much needed privacy, did you not?

Keith Yeah. I fuckin' love the Witterings.

He looks to the jury.

Excuse my language. I like just wittering away in the Witterings, you know what I mean?

Michael (*looking at the jury*) We do know, don't we? And yet on the night in question in this peaceful backwater, Mr Sniderman – a man you barely knew – gatecrashed this private event?

Keith That's correct.

Michael And what did he bring with him to the party?

Keith His pharmacy.

Michael By which you mean –

Keith Drugs. Uppers, downers, stuff to knock you sideways.

Fans gasp.

Michael Quite. And shortly thereafter the police raided?

Keith That's right.

Michael And what happened to Mr Sniderman when the police raided?

Keith He scarpered. Completely disappeared.

Michael Oh! So the police didn't charge him with possession of drugs?

Keith The place was crawling with coppers, and somehow he made a clean getaway.

Michael Odd, no?

Keith Not if the police already knew he was there.

Keith looks pleased with himself. The fans are happy. Allen stands up, all pumped.

Allen Yes!

Block I direct the jury to totally disregard the last statement. It is no defence to this charge.

Lights change.

SCENE FOUR

Courtroom.
Michael and Allen convene outside the courtroom.

Allen What do you think?

Michael I don't know. It would have gone better for us if you could have found Sniderman –

Allen I tried – the man has a thousand different aliases – But I think they got it, don't you? The jury? The connection between the lawsuit and the raid –

Michael Well, I didn't want to stray too far that way, but I had to do something once Richards started playing up. The girl in the rug didn't help matters either.

Allen Not in a roomful of dirty old men, no.

Michael Mr Klein, may I remind you that this is the Law, and prejudice of any kind has no place in it.

Allen Prejudice! I'll tell you who's prejudiced! The judge! He told the jury to ignore any reasonable doubt. What kind of kangaroo court is this? The whole thing's a farce! You know what's really happening here? I'll tell you! These kids, Mick, Keith – they're taking over the world – they're the new aristocracy, man, and the Establishment just don't like it.

Vivek appears.

Vivek The jury are back!

Michael Already?

Michael and Vivek start walking back to the courtroom. Allen follows them.

Allen Is that a good sign? That's a good sign, right?

SCENE FIVE

Courtroom.
  Everyone is still there, including Nigel and Marianne.

Block Bring in the defendants.

  Mick and Keith appear. Block turns to the Clerk.

Mr Clerk. Have the jury reached a unanimous decision?

Clerk They have, Your Honour.

Block In the case of Michael Philip Jagger do they find the defendant guilty or not guilty?

  We hear the opening riff of '(I Can't Get No) Satisfaction'.

Clerk Guilty.

Marianne Noooooooo!

  Mick is open-mouthed in disbelief.

Keith (*quietly*) Fuck me.

  There is shock in the room.

Block And in the case of Keith Richards?

  The opening riff of '(I Can't Get No) Satisfaction' is repeated.

Clerk Horribly guilty.

Fan (*shouts*) They're only saying that cos they've got long hair!

  Music: '(I Can't Get No) Satisfaction' by the Rolling Stones starts.

Michael (*to Vivek*) Let's get out of here!

  Michael and Vivek leave the court.

Allen (*to Michael as he leaves*) Oh you're leaving! Now you've ballsed it all up! What about my boys?! Havers!

Allen exits after him.
  Mick and Keith sing '(I Can't Get No) Satisfaction'. During this Prison Guards come on. Flash bulbs go off as Mick amd Keith are handcuffed by the Guards. They continue to sing as:
  A Journalist runs on with a microphone and accosts Marianne.

Journalist Marianne? What do you think of the verdict? Do you think you should have been on trial today?

Marianne runs off. Nigel follows her.

Nigel Marianne!

During the next, Mick and Keith continue to sing and dance as they are hauled off to prison.
  They are body searched by the Prison Guards. They are handed a towel and a toothbrush each and led off to separate cells. The Guards rip off Mick and Keith's clothes to reveal stripy prison garb underneath. Bars descend. They are well and truly incarcerated. The song ends.

SCENE SIX

White Shutters, kitchen.
   Michael, Carol and Nigel are there. Michael is drinking. He still wears his stiff white collar and barrister suit.

Carol They got sent to prison?! Block actually sent them to prison?

Michael All right. Don't rub it in.

Carol I can't believe it!

Nigel Mick got three months.

Carol No!

Nigel Keith got a year!

Carol But that's terrible! You said they'd get off with a caution.

Michael It's their own fault. They behaved like a couple of clowns.

Nigel How can you say that?

Michael What?

Nigel Your defence was a mess. What on earth did Marianne being in a rug have to do with anything? That was extremely prejudicial.

Michael Oh, you've turned lawyer on me, have you? That's convenient.

Carol All right you two –

Nigel (*to Michael*) You didn't care what happened to them.

Michael Rubbish.

Nigel You looked down on them, Dad. You know you did.

   The doorbell goes.

Carol Who on earth is that?

Michael If it's reporters, tell them I'm not at home.

Carol Reporters?! No one's interested in you, Michael.

She leaves to go and see. Michael takes a big swig of whisky.
  Pause.

Michael Anyway, they weren't exactly innocent. They did take drugs that night. The Stones were stoned.

Nigel So what?! The sentences were totally excessive. You know the real reason why they got sent to prison? Block hated them. You seriously call that justice?

Michael It wasn't jurisprudence's finest moment; I'll give you that. But I'm sure the world can live without them for a year or so – in fact I may have done everyone a favour.

Nigel Oh my God – you are so out of touch! The Stones are adored – they are brilliant musicians. They've got millions of fans. But how would you know? You've never even listened to them.

Michael (*rattled*) I've heard you playing them. I've watched them on television! Cavorting about!

Nigel You didn't see them though. You didn't *see* them for who they really are. Just like you never see me.

A moment and then Carol re-enters. Beside her is Marianne.

Marianne!

Marianne I haven't come to see you, Nigel. It's your dad I wanted to see. Hello, Mr Havers.

Michael Good evening, Miss, er –

Marianne Miss X? Isn't that right? Not faithful any more, am I? No! You said you didn't want to put me in the dock.

You said I wasn't on trial, Mr Havers. But I was, wasn't I? I'm not stupid!

Carol Why don't you sit down, lovey?

Marianne does not sit.

Marianne (*angry*) People think just cos we're in the public eye that we don't have any feelings. That they can print what they like about us, and it won't have an effect. But then millions of people read it and they believe it – they think it's all true –

Carol Oh, that's so mean.

Marianne They don't know me! None of them knows who I really am. They made me out to be a prostitute! I was brought up nicely. I was educated by nuns!

Michael Oh dear oh dear oh dear.

Marianne We trusted you! You said none of this would happen!

Carol Michael, you really are going to have to do something about this. You swan about in your robes, saying clever things – it's all a game to you, but you never think about this! The human cost! This poor girl. Look at her! Look at the state she's in!

Marianne cries.

You poor lamb. Have a tissue.

Carol comforts her and looks pointedly at Michael.

Michael Miss Faithfull. I'm – very – Perhaps I underestimated what effect their – erm, fame would have on the case –

Marianne What good is that now? Mick and Keith are already in prison!! It's too late!!

Carol (*to Marianne*) It's all too much, isn't it? I tell you what's going to happen. You're going to stay here tonight.

Michael What?!

Carol Nigel is going to run you a nice hot bath.

Nigel I am?

Carol It will all feel better in the morning. After a good night's sleep.

Marianne That's so kind of you, Mrs Havers, but I can't stay here –

Carol You must. You need rest. And no one will bother you here. We're in the middle of nowhere.

Marianne That is true.

Pause.

Are you sure?

Carol I am certain. In fact, you can stay as long as you want. You need to be out of the public eye right now. Have you eaten anything?

Marianne I'm not hungry. Really.

Carol All right. Nigel, take Marianne up and show her where everything is.

Nigel stands up.

Nigel Yes, sure.

Marianne looks at him.

Marianne Looks like I'm having a sleepover!

Nigel Yes.

Nigel turns to the audience.

(*To the audience.*) This is the best day of my life.

Michael Hang on a minute! I don't think this is a good idea –

Carol I don't care what you think.

Michael What?!

Pause.

(*Faltering.*) What if – I mean – if – what –

Nigel (*to the audience*) Look at him! I've never seen him like this before.

Carol (*to Nigel and Marianne*) Off you go, you two.

Marianne Thank you, Mrs Havers.

Carol Carol, please.

Marianne Carol.

They leave. Michael is staring at Carol.

Carol Why are you looking at me like that?

Michael Have you gone completely insane? She can't stay here!

Carol Of course, she can.

Michael What about Nigel?

Carol What about Nigel?

Michael You saw how he is around her. He's sixteen –

Carol Seventeen!

Michael Seventeen years old. It might stir something in him – something he can't control –

Carol It looks like you're the only one who's getting stirred up.

Michael I've got to work tonight. I've got to deal with this bloody mess – I can't have her distracting me!

Carol Oh, pull yourself together. She's not interested in you.

She looks in a drawer for a pill bottle.

I think I'll give her something to calm her down.

Michael You're giving her drugs? Have you lost your mind?! You can't give her drugs – I forbid it! What drugs?

Carol Just a bit of diazey . . .

Michael Diazepam! What else have you got stashed away? Magic mushrooms? Benzedrine?

She takes a pill out of the bottle and then leaves it on the table.

Carol Yes, I think there's a bottle of that at the back.

Michael Benzedrine!

Carol Of course!

Michael This is utterly irresponsible –

Carol Oh, shut up, you old fart.

Michael What if the papers got hold of this? I'd be disbarred.

Carol Well, maybe that would be a good thing.

Michael I beg your pardon?

Carol You need to care about *people*, Michael. People are what matter, not the bloody Law.

She goes to go and turns back.

And you can sleep in your study tonight.

She exits. Michael is left. He realises he has lost all control of this situation. He pours himself a glass of whisky. Then he takes a pill out of the diazepam bottle and swallows it. Michael exits with the glass and goes into his study.

SCENE SEVEN

Michael's study, White Shutters. Night.
   Michael huffs and puffs as he sits. He looks at the wig on his desk. On its stand. He picks it up and puts it on. For comfort. He finds that it is itchy. He itches his head. A moment and then he realises that his stiff white collar is far too tight. He can't breathe. He tugs at it to loosen it a bit.
   He switches on the radio. He listens.

Radio Announcer (*'BBC English'*) Protestors are taking to the streets tonight in opposition to the lengthy jail sentences meted out in court today to Rolling Stones members Keith Richards and Mick Jagger.

   Michael turns the volume up.

Violent demonstrations are currently taking place outside the offices of the *News of the World* in Fleet Street. And there are reports coming in that protestors have now broken into the grounds of the Inner Temple and are holding a vigil there.

Michael Oh, good God!

   He gives up. Lays his head on his desk.
   Lights change. Music starts.
   Marianne appears in a virginal white robe, flowers in her hair. She starts to sing to him. 'As Tears Go By' by the Rolling Stones. The other women in the ensemble join her and harmonise. They are dressed as hippies too and carry candles. Michael looks up in complete wonderment. He is totally seduced.
   At the end of the song, they all exit, humming.

No, don't go – stay, please!

   Michael is left. He wonders if he is about to cry? Surely not. He takes out a hanky and blows his nose. He stands up. He throws off his wig. He undoes the three fiddly little buttons at the front of his stiff collar with some difficulty. Finally, he can breathe. He ruffles his hair. He decides. He leaves.

SCENE EIGHT

White Shutters, kitchen.
   Carol is preparing breakfast. Nigel helps her lay the table.

Nigel Where's Dad?

Carol (*smiling*) I have no idea, Jelly. I'm giving him the silent treatment till he remembers his humanity again.

> *She puts the newspaper on the table. Marianne enters the kitchen wearing a T-shirt of Philip's and little else. Nigel looks at her and then picks up* The Times *newspaper that Carol has just laid on the table.*

Good morning, darling. Did you sleep well?

Marianne Like a dream.

Carol Oh good.

Marianne Morning, Nigel.

Nigel Yes. Hello.

> *He starts reading* The Times.

Carol Are you hungry? I'm making an omelette. Mama Cass laid me three beautiful big eggs today –

Marianne Mama Cass?

Nigel My mother keeps chickens.

Carol My babies.

Marianne I wish I had a mum like you!

Carol What a lovely thing to say! You know I always wished I had a daughter. One can get so outnumbered.

Marianne Maybe me and Mick will get some chickens. Live on a little farm – like you . . . One day.

Carol Of course you will! If you want to. Why not?

Marianne My dad started a commune in Oxfordshire. They say it's like having one big family. But for me it was like having no family at all.

Carol (*touched*) Oh dear! Yes, I can see how that could be difficult.

Marianne I wish I'd grown up somewhere like this.

Nigel (*showing the paper*) Oh my God, you two! You have to read this. The editorial today. It's all about the case! The headline is: 'Who Breaks a Butterfly on a Wheel'? What does that mean?

Carol It's a quote, I think. Dryden or Pope – one of those old boys –

Marianne What does it say?

Nigel It's basically saying Mick Jagger is delicate – like a butterfly. And that the justice system tried to crush him.

Marianne That's true!

Nigel It says there's been a terrible miscarriage of justice.

Carol Well, isn't that good news?! Someone talking sense at last. Hopefully your father will be able to use that to his advantage.

Marianne I hope so. I can't stop thinking about Mick. All alone in his cell. He must be so scared.

Carol Best not dwell on that. You need to keep yourself busy. What are you two going to do today?

Marianne I've got some lines to learn. For an audition. Perhaps you can help me, Nigel?

Carol Oh yes, he'd love that!

Nigel Yes, I would.

Carol smiles at them both.

Carol Excellent!

SCENE NINE

Chambers, Michael's office. Day.
Michael sits reading The Times *editorial. Vivek is there with him.*

Michael This *is* excellent! An establishment paper like *The Times* coming out to bat for them.

Vivek Have you heard how the boys are getting on in prison?

Michael Apparently Jagger passed a comfortable night playing Scrabble with his cellmate.

Vivek Oh, that's nice. He is a very refined person, I think.

Michael Richards on the other hand was greeted like the prodigal son. Rattling of bars and widespread ululation ensued when he walked in. It appears he's found his tribe! Not that we will tell anyone that.

Vivek No?

Michael No. We shall say that whilst incarcerated they are under constant threat and scared for their lives!

Vivek Oh, good thinking!

A knock on the door and Daphne enters.

Daphne Excuse me, Mr Havers –

Michael Ah, Daphne my dear. Come in! How are you?

Pause.

Daphne (*shocked*) I – erm. I'm fine, Mr Havers.

He is looking at her earnestly.

Michael Yes. You are! You are fine. And your hair is looking very – firm. Nice and firm.

Daphne touches the back of her heavily lacquered helmet of hair, in a state of shock.

Daphne Thank you.

Michael You're most welcome.

She turns to leave, turns back.

Daphne Oh, I almost forgot – Mr Klein is here to see you.

Michael Marvellous – send him in!

She leaves.

Vivek If I may say so, sir, you seem different today.

Michael Do I? In what way?

Vivek I don't know. Somehow your vibrational energy has changed –

Michael (*pleased*) Has it?

Vivek I am thinking your chakras must have come into alignment.

Michael Good stuff!

Suddenly Allen bursts into the room.

Allen You're going to have to give me a very good reason why I don't fire you right now and find myself another lawyer.

Michael Mr Klein! Please don't work yourself up into a state. How are your blood sugar levels? Do you need a shot?

Allen I'll give you a goddamned shot! I've been on the phone all morning to the US – the Rolling Stones tour is going to be cancelled – turns out they won't let jailbirds in!

Michael Deep breaths now. It's all under control.

Allen Is it?!

Michael I have already applied for bail. You heard about last night's riots no doubt –

Vivek And today's editorial in *The Times*.

Michael Public opinion is on our side! On the back of which I am going to ask for permission to appeal the sentences.

Allen And how long will that take?

Michael You can't rush the Law, I'm afraid, Mr Klein. But we have a very strong case.

Allen That's what you said last time.

Michael Chichester let the side down, I'm afraid. The whole thing was a farce. I shall say that the young men's fame was held against them –

Allen And what about the *News of the World*?

Michael Well. We don't want to go too far –

Allen I don't know what it is with the press in this country. You let them get away with murder.

Pause.

Michael You need to understand that we need concrete evidence of the *News of the World*'s involvement.

Allen Well then let's get it!

SCENE TEN

White Shutters.
  Nigel and Marianne run on as Hamlet and Ophelia. They carry scripts.

Nigel (*as Hamlet*) Where's your father?

Marianne (*flatly, as Ophelia*) At home, my lord.

Nigel Let the doors be shut upon him – that he may play the fool nowhere but in's own house –

Marianne (*interrupting*) Oh Nigel! Can we stop? I can't do this.

Nigel What? Yes, you can! If you can do Chekhov, then you can do Shakespeare!

Marianne It's not that. I don't even know if I want to be an actress any more –

  Pause.

Nigel What's wrong?

Marianne Mick doesn't want me to go for this audition.

Nigel Why not?

Marianne He needs me. He doesn't want me going off. He's angry –

  Pause.

I think I just need to support Mick. He's the one with the real talent –

Nigel Nonsense!

Marianne Everything's changed between him and me since Redlands. It's almost like he believes the things they write about me.

Nigel But why would he do that? Surely he knows the papers are full of lies.

Marianne You'd think. I don't know. Maybe he's growing tired of me.

Nigel That's impossible.

Pause.

Marianne Oh Nigel, I'm just not in the mood for acting.

Nigel Why don't we just run through it once more?

Marianne Do we have to?

Nigel Just so you know the lines at least. In case you change your mind.

Pause.

Marianne Okay. Go on then.

Nigel From 'Let the doors be shut'?

She nods.

Let the doors be shut upon him, that he may play the fool nowhere but in's own house. Farewell.

Marianne O, help him, you sweet heavens.

Nigel is in full flow now. He already half knows the lines.

Nigel If thou dost marry, I'll give thee this plague for thy dowry. Be thou as chaste as ice, as pure as snow, thou shalt not escape calumny. Get thee to a nunnery, go. Farewell.

Marianne Nigel Havers!

She looks at him, amazed. He stops.

Nigel What?

Marianne You dark horse!

Pause.

Why didn't you tell me?

Nigel What?

Marianne You're an actor!

Nigel I must confess I do love it. It's basically my life.

Marianne That's wonderful! You're going to be an actor!

Nigel Oh no. No. I'll never be an actor.

Marianne Why not?

Nigel My dad. He won't let me. He thinks the theatre is stupid. The only thing he believes in is the Law. I can't even tell him. I'm too scared –

Carol enters. She carries a basket of washing.

Carol You can tell me.

Nigel Mum! Were you eavesdropping?

Carol It's a mother's prerogative.

Marianne Did you hear him act, Carol? He's brilliant, isn't he brilliant?

Carol Of course he is. He takes after me.

Nigel What?

Carol puts the washing basket down on the table. She starts to fold the laundry during the next.

Carol Before I married your father, I had dreams of becoming an actress.

Nigel I didn't know that –

Carol I've never told you boys. I was a thrilling Titania – at school, of course.

Marianne I can see that.

Carol Thank you, dear . . . I even thought about drama school. But then I met your father.

Nigel He stopped you?

Carol I stopped myself. Women didn't have careers really – not in those days. Oh, I don't regret it. I really don't. Your father was a midshipman in the Navy then. He looked so handsome in his uniform. I wanted so badly to be married . . . Then I had your brother and you, of course. And now I wouldn't wish it any different.

She looks at Nigel.

And the point is, I wasn't as good as you are.

Pause.

Nigel, I do think that when one has this thing – this talent – inside of one, one does have a duty to try and let it out.

Marianne Your mum's right.

Carol There's no point in being unhappy, love –

Nigel But what about Dad?

Pause.

Carol You will have to face up to him at some point.

Nigel I've tried. But he doesn't listen. He only hears what he wants to hear.

Pause.

Carol True. Perhaps I can soften him up for you a bit. The thing about your father is he doesn't like to be told things. But if I can make him think it was his idea all along –

Marianne Carol, I like your style!

Carol Hmmm. And the funny thing is, he thinks *he's* the best lawyer in the family.

SCENE ELEVEN

The Garrick Club.
 Michael enters. Cecil is sitting at a table, drinking a brandy.

Michael Good afternoon, pater.

Cecil I see you totally cocked up the Stones case then, son. You went at it all the wrong way. I don't know why you didn't consult with me –

Michael I knew you'd be like this. Can't we be civil? Just talk about the weather before you have a go at me?

Suddenly a theatrical voice booms out, as Block appears.

Block 'You blocks, you Stones, you worse than senseless things!'

Michael Oh God.

Cecil (*stage whisper*) It's buggering Block. Judge Block! Right behind you.

Michael I know who it is, Dad.

Michael turns round to greet Block.

Your Honour. Fancy meeting you here.

Block *Julius Caesar*, Act One, Scene One. Got a certain ring of truth to it, hasn't it?

Michael I'm familiar with the quotation, Your Honour.

Michael looks up and nods at the doorman.

And I think you'll be familiar with my guests today too.

Michael puts his arm out to beckon two figures who are suddenly standing in the doorway.
 They are Mick and Keith, in their modish finery.
Mick and Keith enter the gentlemen's club like strutting peacocks. They are accompanied by Allen.

Cecil (*tickled*) The boys are out! You got them out!

Michael Of course I got them out.

Mick and Keith treat the length of the room as their catwalk.

Cecil Oh, what fun!

They draw level with Block.

Mick All right, Blocky?

Keith How you diddlin'?

Block is aghast. He turns back to Michael.

Block What on earth do you mean by this vulgar display? In the Garrick, of all places! This is worse than having women in here! And believe you me, we will *never* have women here!

Block turns to the doorman.

Doorman! May I enquire if these personages are members? If not, would you kindly eject them –

Michael (*calmly, elegantly*) No. They are not members. They are my guests. But you know – perhaps they ought to be members. I've always felt the rules here were a little draconian.

Cecil I second that. We could do with some young blood. What do you say?

Keith (*mock posh*) I do own a castle, after all.

An irate Block looks at them and then storms out. Michael turns to Mick, Keith and Allen.

Michael Won't you take a seat, gentlemen?

Allen Nicely played, Havers.

Cecil Oh! I do love a scene! Hello, boys!

Michael Gentlemen, this is my father. Sir Cecil Havers.

Cecil Do call me Bongo. It's what my grandsons call me. I say, well done, Michael. Cocking a snoop at the old guard!

Keith Yeah, two fingers to the old git – eh, Bongo?

Cecil laughs, delighted.

Cecil Absolutely!

Michael gestures to a waiter who arrives with a bottle of champagne and some glasses.

I say, boys! Did Michael ever tell you I met the Beatles once? Nice enough, but a bit namby-pamby. Nothing compared to you rocker boys!

Keith You're making me blush, Bongo.

Michael starts to pour the champagne.

Mick Are we celebrating something then?

Michael An appeal date has been set. And don't worry, we're going to win this time.

Allen I'll drink to that –

Michael But also I – I wanted to apologise to you gentlemen. I underestimated you. I actually had no idea how important you are –

Keith And we thought you were a right arsehole.

Michael So this time round, let's meet each other halfway, eh?

Michael takes his glass and raises it in a toast.

To freedom. Yes?

Cecil Well played, my boy, well played. I'll drink to that! To freedom!

The men all raise their glasses. To Freedom.

SCENE ELEVEN B

Nigel walks on. He carries an envelope. He addresses the audience.

Nigel (*to the audience*) Do you know why I love the Stones? Aside from the music, I mean? They don't ask permission to be who they are. They knew who they were right from the beginning and they just stuck to it. They never apologised. They never let anything stand in their way. I need to be more like that. But I'm not. Not really. I think the problem is – and please don't tell anyone this – but I still want to please my dad. I want his approval. I don't know why. It's really the most rotten luck.

He shows the audience the envelope.

This is my application to drama school. I should just post it, shouldn't I? What the hell? Okay. I'm going to do it! Break a leg – and all that.

He leaves.

SCENE ELEVEN C

The Garrick Club.
Mick, Keith and Allen exit the Club, led by Michael.

Michael Thank you again, gentlemen, I'll be in touch.

A journalist runs on with a camera. It is Derek Carter, late thirties, a London hack.

Carter Mick! Keith! Glad to be out of prison? Smile for the camera, eh?

Carter starts taking photos of them. Click, click, click.

Mick It's Carter! The journalist who started all this mess.

Keith Oi, Carter, what the fuck you playing at?

Carter Don't be like that, fellas. I'm doing you a favour! Keeping you in the news!

Keith sees red.

Keith I'm gonna punch his fucking lights out.

Michael hastens after him, pulls him back.

Michael No, Keith. You do not want to get re-arrested, believe me.

Carter is still taking photos.

I'll deal with him.

Michael goes to Carter. The others watch and wait.

What do you think you're doing?

Carter Me? I'm just doing my job, mate. Not breaking any laws. Freedom of speech and all that!

Michael Can't you see you've done enough damage with all the lies you've printed –

Carter That's what sells the papers though.

Michael I want you to leave my clients alone now. I'm asking you nicely –

Carter is starting to walk away, laughing.

Carter Sorry, mate. No can do. If they didn't want to be in the papers, they shouldn't have been famous, should they?

He walks off jauntily. The others join Michael.

Mick You see this is what we get every day.

Allen You think this is justice?

Michael The problem is freedom of the press is enshrined in the Law.

Pause.

But God dammit, you're right, this is not justice. I'm going to make that man stand in the Appeal Trial.

Allen You mean it?

Michael Yes. I do. Together, we're going to take on the *News of the World*.

SCENE ELEVEN D

The others exit as Michael strides into the auditorium. The Male Usher is there with his ice-cream/sweets tray. He has newspapers for sale as well.

Male Usher Evening. What can I do for you, guvnor?

Michael I'll have a *Standard*. And a Mars bar please.

Male Usher You want a Marianne Faithfull? Life in the old dog yet, eh?

The Male Usher goes to hand it to him.

Michael On second thoughts I'll leave it.

Michael goes to go. Turns back.

I happen to be acquainted with Miss Faithfull. And I want you to know that she is a very nice, rather sensitive young woman. Educated by nuns, did you know that? Don't believe everything you read in the papers, eh?

Michael walks away.

SCENE TWELVE

White Shutters, kitchen.
   Carol is engaged in domestic chores as Michael enters.

Michael All right, dear?

Carol Oh, what do you care?

   He stops. A little scared.

Michael Carol? Is it that time of the month again?

Carol NO IT IS NOT.

Michael Then what is it, my dear?

   Pause.

Carol My father used to take me butterfly hunting when I was little, did I ever tell you that?

Michael No –

Carol Well I didn't enjoy it one bit. Chasing after that beautiful little thing with a net. And then locking it up in a killing jar. That's what he called it you know. A killing jar. He put chloroform on a piece of cotton at the bottom. The way it flapped its poor little wings before it died! How frantic it was. I can't bear to think of it, even now.

   Pause.

(*Intently.*) Michael. Beautiful young things need to fly free. Don't you agree?

Michael You know I hate it when you talk in code to me.

Carol Come on!

Michael Are you talking about the boys?

Carol Yes!

Michael You don't have to worry – Mick and Keith are fine –

Carol Oh Michael. I despair. I really do.

Pause.

Michael Good God! Carol, I hope you don't feel trapped – with me, I mean. You know I couldn't live without you.

Carol I know.

Michael You're as beautiful to me now as the first day I clapped eyes on you –

Carol Am I?

Michael Oh, my dear . . . I don't appreciate you enough, do I?

Carol No, you don't.

Pause.

Michael Carol. I know I'm not as young as I once was. But I thought – I thought we might retire early tonight.

Pause.

Carol The night before a big case? Are you sure?

Michael Absolutely sure.

Pause.

But only if you're amenable?

Carol I could certainly be persuaded.

Michael Persuasion is my strong suit.

He goes to exit. She stops.

What?

Carol Would you like me to wear a fug rug?

He laughs. Stops.

Michael Do we have a fur rug?

Carol We've got that old crochet blanket your mother knitted.

Michael That'll do nicely.

They exit.

SCENE THIRTEEN

Chambers.
The day dawns.
The Inner Temple prepares. The secretaries type in perfect time. Vivek goes back and forth with papers.
Michael is sitting at his desk. Making notes. Daphne comes in discreetly with his barrister's robe. Michael is a little on edge.

Michael Ah, Daphne! You made sure Savile Row sent the suits?

Daphne Yes, Mr Havers.

Michael Navy silk for Mick and charcoal worsted for Keith –

Daphne Yes, Mr Havers.

Michael You sent them both to Redlands?

Daphne They have the suits, Mr Havers.

Michael Good. Good.

She exits as Vivek enters carrying a pile of briefs.

Vivek Lord Chief Justice Parker is confirmed at the Royal Courts of Justice today.

Michael Parker. That should be okay. He's an impartial chap. And he knows we want to call a new witness?

Vivek Yes! And there's a full-page advertisement in *The Times* today, saying that cannabis should be legalised –

Michael I'll look at it later.

Vivek And Parliament is tabling a debate into the medical benefits of soft drug use. This case has raised some serious issues.

Michael Yes, all right, stop talking now.

Pause.

Vivek Are you all right, Mr Havers?

Michael Just a little nervous. Sorry, Vivek. Ridiculous. Heart pumping away. Haven't felt like this for years.

Vivek Maybe that's a good thing?

Michael Do you think?

Pause.

Vivek I'll leave you to prepare then.

Michael Best had.

Michael is left alone. He stands up. He reverently takes down his barrister's robe. Puts it on. He performs a little personal ritualised warm-up. A small knock. Daphne enters again.

Daphne The gentlemen have arrived, Mr Havers.

Michael What are you waiting for, Daphne? Send them straight in.

Daphne Very good, sir.

After a moment Mick enters in a beautiful navy suit, followed by Keith in his equally swish grey number.

Michael Well, look at you both. Very dapper. You look almost –

Keith Respectable?

Michael I wouldn't go that far. But you'll pass.

Mick Thanks, Dad!

Pause.

Michael (*touched*) Ah! Yes. Ha ha. Good. Well. Take a seat, my boys – we just have to go through a few last-minute things. Now I want you to really look the judge in the eye – remind him you're not just rock stars – you're vulnerable human beings –

Mick Gotcha.

A knock at the door.

Michael Oh, for goodness' sake! What is it now?

Daphne Mr Havers –

Michael Can't you see we're working?

Daphne Yes, I'm sorry, sir. But it's your son –

Nigel pushes past her into the room.

Michael Nigel?!

Nigel Dad.

Michael Can't you see we're busy –

Nigel Oh, hello, Mick. Hello, Keith.

Keith Hey, Nige.

Mick Marianne's told us all about you.

Nigel I wouldn't have interrupted you, but I need to talk to my dad.

Michael Whatever it is, it'll have to wait till later –

Nigel It can't wait any longer! Today's the day!

Michael What are you talking about?

Nigel I've got an audition. For drama school. The RADA, Dad! The Royal Academy of Dramatic Art. I'm going to leave school and train to be an actor –

Michael looks at Nigel. Mick and Keith exchange glances. Michael turns to Mick and Keith.

Michael I'm terribly sorry, gentlemen, will you excuse me for a moment?

They nod. Michael draws Nigel to one side.

Did you honestly think this was an appropriate time to share your future plans with me?

Nigel But the audition is today, Dad!

Michael And today is the appeal! Probably the most important date in my career so far –

Nigel I'm not trying to annoy you. Really, I'm not. But there's nothing wrong with acting as a career – Mum doesn't mind. She's happy for me. The point is, I've been trying to tell you for weeks –

Michael (*shutting it down*) The point is, I'm at work, Nigel. And I really do not appreciate being ambushed like this when I am working.

Pause.

Nigel The Law always comes first, doesn't it, Dad?

Nigel leaves. Michael returns to Mick and Keith.

Michael I'm very sorry about that. On to more important business!

Mick All he wants is your approval. You know that, right?

Michael Yes, well, we don't need to concern ourselves with that –

Mick My dad wasn't keen on me leaving college and getting into music either. But I told him – it's my life, not yours.

Keith My dad was a factory worker. I'm like a changeling to him. We don't speak no more.

Michael I'm sorry to hear that. Anyway –

Mick You know people often ask us – how did you become famous rock stars? And I say rock and roll doesn't come from here –

Mick points at his head.

Keith It comes from here.

Keith grabs his crotch.

Mick And it comes from here too.

Mick touches his heart.

If it's in you, it's in you.

Keith If your Nige wants to be an actor, he'll be an actor. Nothing you say will stop him.

Mick And if you're not careful. You'll lose him.

Pause.

Michael Right.

SCENE FOURTEEN

Outside RADA.
  Nigel walks on with Marianne.

Marianne Who cares what he thinks anyway? This is not about your dad. It's about you.

Nigel But it's going to be really embarrassing if I don't get in. Oh my God! He'll have a field day!

Marianne Hey, Havers! Forget about your dad. Concentrate on what you're about to do.

Nigel I'm so nervous, Marianne!

Marianne Just do your piece like we rehearsed it.

Nigel I wish you could come with me.

Marianne Me too. But I really should show my face at the Appeal Court. It's an important day for Mick.

Nigel Oh no, absolutely.

  A cool young Drama Student in a beret passes them, pauses a moment.

Drama Student Looking for auditions? Straight on.

Nigel Thanks.

Drama Student Good luck!

  Nigel turns back to Marianne.

Marianne Break a leg, kiddo.

Nigel Thanks.

  He exits.

Drama Student Sorry to bother you, but – are you Marianne Faithfull?

  Pause.

Marianne I really don't know any more.

After a moment she exits a different way.

SCENE FIFTEEN

The Court of Appeal.
  The Court Clerk stands in front of Carter, who is in the stand.

Clerk State your name for the record please.

Carter Derek Carter.

Michael steps forward.

Michael And what is your profession, Mr Carter?

Carter Senior reporter at the *News of the World*.

Michael On the fifth of February of this year the *News of the World* published a story about Mick Jagger that was blatantly untrue. You accused him of taking cocaine, when in fact it was Brian Jones who consumed the drug –

Carter The story was true to the best of my knowledge –

Michael But it still wasn't *true*, was it?

Carter It was a case of mistaken identity.

Michael Which makes it a lie. And in response Mr Jagger initiated libel proceedings. Which made your editor very angry. Which then forced you to fabricate another story to exact your revenge –

Carter I didn't fabricate anything –

Michael No? Can you explain then why, merely a week later, the West Sussex Constabulary, acting on a tip-off, raided Redlands, Mr Richards' home.

Carter I don't know –

Michael Really? But you were hiding in the bushes when they arrived, weren't you?

Carter I – don't recall –

Vivek hands a newspaper to Michael. Michael displays the front page of the News of the World. *Photos of Mick, Keith and Marianne outside Redlands.*

Michael It was you who took these photos, wasn't it? They are credited to you.

Carter (*mumbles*) Yes.

Michael I'm sorry I don't think we heard that.

Carter Yes I did.

Michael And then you told the police that there would be drugs at the party that night. And you knew that, didn't you, because you had in fact sent David Sniderman, aka the Acid King, to Redlands to supply those drugs, had you not? For which service you paid him?

Pause.

Carter Yes.

Michael Thank you, Mr Carter. That will be all.

Carter You don't understand! It's my job!

Michael turns on him angrily.

Michael Oh, it's your job? That is the job of a decent journalist, is it? To create a narrative where there is none? To throw innocent people under the bus? Just to sell a few papers?

Carter It's my job to hold famous people to account.

Michael (*angry*) You weren't holding them to account! You were holding them to ransom – so that you wouldn't have to pay out for the lies that you'd already printed about them! I sincerely hope that one day someone holds *you* to account, sir. You and your tawdry newspaper.

Pause.

But until that time, I have nothing further.

SCENE SIXTEEN

Stage, RADA.
Nigel walks onto the stage uncertainly. A voice from the audience. The Principal is sitting there.

Principal Name?

Nigel Havers. Nigel Havers.

Pause.

Should I start?

Principal In your own time, Mr Havers.

Pause.

Nigel Erm, just to say I'm going to be doing Portia's speech from *The Merchant of Venice*.

Principal You are aware that Portia is a girl's part?

Nigel Yes, I know. But Portia is disguised as a man when she speaks – and of course in Shakespeare's time she would have been played by a man. And I thought the speech would suit me. Because of my age.

Principal Very persuasive. You'd make a very good lawyer.

Nigel shakes his head.

Nigel No, thank you.

Principal All right, Mr Havers. Show us what you've got.

SCENE SEVENTEEN

The Court of Appeal/RADA.
Michael steps forward to give his closing address. Mick and Keith stand behind him.

Michael Two young men stand before you today. Two boys – who met at school and found friendship through their shared love of music. It's not a traditional route to take through life and nor is it an easy one. But thanks to their extraordinary talent, many people in the world love them. And we should be proud of that. For who are we as a society without our artists?

Pause.

I have two boys myself. One of them will be a lawyer like me. And the other –

He looks at Carol.

It is very difficult in life to admit that you are wrong. That you have made a mistake. That you have treated someone – too harshly.

Pause.

But sometimes that is exactly what we must do. For what does Shakespeare say:

Lights up on Nigel. His audition.

Nigel
The quality of mercy is not strained.
It droppeth as the gentle rain from heaven
Upon the place beneath. It is twice blest;
It blesseth him that gives and him that takes.

Lights up on the Court of Appeal.

Michael
'Tis mightiest in the mightiest; it becomes
The thronèd monarch better than his crown:

His sceptre shows the force of temporal power,
The attribute to awe and majesty,
Wherein doth sit the dread and fear of kings.

Michael *and* **Nigel**
But mercy is above this sceptred sway;
It is enthronèd in the hearts of kings,
It is an attribute to God himself;
And earthly power doth then show likest God's
When mercy seasons justice.

It is the end of the trial. Mick and Keith come forward to shake Michael's hand.

Keith Nice one, Mike!

Mick You played a blinder.

Vivek, Carol and Cecil come forward to congratulate Michael.

Vivek Stunning result, Michael!

Cecil Chip off the old block, son!

Allen is there too. They all shake Michael's hand. Slap him on the back. Michael is somewhat subdued.

Allen Michael Havers, what can I say? I never doubted you for a moment. Thanks to you the Stones are gonna roll again! What do you say to a tour in the US of A, boys?

Mick *and* **Keith** Hell yeah!

They stay in a huddle round Michael. Marianne is waiting a little behind them.

Marianne Hey, Mick! Congratulations. You did it!

Pause.

Mick I didn't know you were here.

Marianne Of course I'm here. Where else would I be?

Mick I dunno.

Pause.

Marianne Mick? What is it?

Mick Nothing!

Marianne Have I done something wrong?

Mick Don't ruin the vibe, yeah? We'll talk later.

She nods and backs away from him.

Allen Well, we need to celebrate!

Vivek There's going to be a party back at the Inner Temple. Who's coming? Mick?

Mick Try and stop me.

Cecil Did someone say party?!

There are cheers. They all exit. Marianne trails behind Mick.
Michael and Carol are left. They look at each other.

Michael Nigel. You've been trying to tell me for weeks –

Carol nods.

Michael I need to put this right, don't I? Where's the audition?

Carol RADA. Gower Street –

Michael Do you think I'm too late?

Carol I don't know. Go now! *Run!*

Michael exits at speed through the auditorium.
Lights up on Nigel.

Nigel (*to the audience*) So he runs to find me. All the way from the Royal Courts of Justice. Still in his robes, mind. Plus it's raining.

The Female Usher hands Michael an umbrella.

Michael Thank you.

Nigel In his haste to get there he gets lost once or twice.

Michael turns back on himself in the auditorium.

Michael Damn it! Sorry! Excuse me!

Michael goes a different route through the auditorium.

Nigel (*to the audience*) Down Drury Lane. Past theatre after theatre. The Royal Opera House. The Shaftesbury. The Aldwych. Down Coptic Street. Bloomsbury Street. Across Bedford Square and on to Gower Street. He can't find it at first.

Michael (*to an audience member*) Excuse me, I'm terribly sorry. I'm looking for the Royal Academy of Dramatic Art. Up ahead? Thank you very much.

Michael arrives at RADA, breathless. Abandons the umbrella.

Nigel (*to the audience*) He puts a girdle round the earth. For me.

Nigel turns to face him.

Michael Ni— Nigel!

He pauses to catch his breath.

Nigel Dad?!

Michael One moment!

Pause.

I – I just wanted – to be here – to wish you luck –

Nigel I've done it. The audition. It's over.

Pause.

Michael Oh. How did it go?

Nigel Okay, I think.

They look at each other. After a pause, Michael finds the courage to speak.

Michael The thing is, Nigel, I've lived my life in a very straight line. Westminster, Cambridge and then the Bar. It's what my father taught me – and I didn't have the imagination or the courage to deviate from that course. I made the Law my life . . . but at times I see it may have been a life sentence. It has taken me away from the things that really matter . . . I have tried my hardest to be a good father. To teach you and your brother how to be men. But I see that in many ways I have fallen short. I have failed to see, really see, the people who mean the most to me in the world. And for that I am deeply sorry.

Nigel stares at his father. At this moment the Principal comes onto the stage.

Principal (*to Nigel*) Still here, Havers? That's it for today, I'm afraid.

Michael Good day to you, are you the principal? I'm Nigel's father.

Principal How do you do?

They shake his hands.

Michael How did he get on?

Principal I'm afraid I can't comment on that. We'll be sending out letters in due course.

The Principal moves off. Turns back. Looks at Nigel.

But Havers, don't whatever you do cut that hair of yours. It's going to make you millions.

He exits.

Nigel Oh my God, Dad! Do you think that means –

Michael They'll be lucky to have you.

Michael smiles.

I should have said this to you a long time ago – but – I am immensely proud of you.

Pause.

Anyway, that's it. I'm not someone who hugs, I'm afraid. It's one of my life's great regrets –

Nigel ignores this and runs and throws his arms around him. They embrace.

SCENE EIGHTEEN

Chambers.
We hear sounds of a party off. Marianne is smoking alone outside. A few of the Chambers staff pass her in party mode. Vivek, Frieda, Sheila, Daphne.
Nigel comes to find Marianne.

Nigel Marianne? I've been looking for you. Are you okay?

She looks at him. A false brightness.

Marianne Of course. Hey. Well done you. I hear it went well.

Nigel Thanks to you.

Marianne Nothing to do with me. You're gonna be a great actor one day. I just know it.

Nigel The party's started. Shall we go in together?

Pause.

Marianne It's not my party.

Nigel What?

Marianne Mick and Keith got off today, but I didn't.

Nigel Don't say that.

She stubs her cigarette out. Pulls herself together. She turns to go.

Where are you going?

She looks at him and then runs back to him and gives him a hug. A sisterly hug.

Marianne I love you, Havers, Nigel Havers.

Nigel (*tearful*) Don't go!

Marianne (*emotional*) It's okay. Really. I'll just have to find myself another party, won't I?

She leaves through the auditorium. Nigel watches her go. As he does he begins to sing 'Ruby Tuesday' by the Rolling Stones. After the first verse, Marianne stops and sings back to him. Finally they sing the chorus together. Marianne leaves. Carol is suddenly there.

Carol Nigel?

Nigel She'll be all right, won't she?

Carol I don't know, son. I very much hope so.

Nigel I need to do something – I need to help her –

Carol It's her journey. You have to let her go.

Pause.

Come here.

They embrace.

My sensitive boy.

She pulls apart from him first.

But you mustn't be sad tonight. We have to celebrate your success. Run along now. Your father's waiting for you in his office.

Nigel What? He hasn't changed his mind, has he?

Carol Go and see.

He looks at her and then nods and goes off.

SCENE NINETEEN

Michael's office.
Michael is sitting, smoking a cigar and drinking a victory glass of whisky. Nigel enters.

Michael Ah, Nigel! Just the chap.

Nigel You wanted to see me.

Michael I have something for you.

Michael opens his drawer and takes out Marianne's tin of hash.

Here.

Nigel What is it?

Michael Well, open it.

Nigel takes the tin and opens it.

Nigel Is this? Dad! Where did you get this?!

Michael I'm afraid I can't reveal my sources.

Nigel takes the joint she made out. Looks at it.

I was told that it is Turkish in origin. But personally, I'm not so sure.

Nigel You can't keep this here!

Michael No! That's why I thought that you would know better than I do how to – deal – with it . . .

He smiles at his son. Nigel looks at the tin. Then at the audience.

Nigel (*to the audience*) Now before you go jumping to any conclusions, I can't say for sure that my father knew that this was cannabis. And if he did know, he certainly wasn't asking me to smoke it. And even if at some unspecified point in the future I did actually smoke it, you know, don't you, that I certainly didn't inhale?

Michael Nigel? Who on earth are you talking to?

Nigel The audience.

Michael The – what?

Michael looks at the audience. He sees them for the first time.

Good God! Have they been there the whole time?

Nigel nods.

Watching me?

Nigel nods. Michael look at the audience again and starts to enjoy his moment in the spotlight.

Well, hello there!

Nigel Dad! I'm the actor in the family. Not you.

Michael (*pulling himself together*) Quite right.

Music: Intro to 'Jumpin' Jack Flash' by the Rolling Stones.

(*To Nigel.*) Well, son, it's never too late to enjoy a misspent youth. Time to party, don't you think?

Mick and Keith enter and sing 'Jumpin' Jack Flash'.
Nigel starts to dance like Mick, to his dad's great amusement.

The rest of the Chambers join the party. They all dance. Vivek and Daphne. Carol and Allen. Cecil does a little solo. Michael takes over from Allen and dances with Carol. Twirls her round. Tips her back.
The Stones strut their stuff.
The song ends.
Lights fade.
The End.